Comments on other *Amazing Stories* from readers & reviewers

"Tightly written volumes filled with lots of wit and humour about famous and infamous Canadians."
Eric Shackleton, *The Globe and Mail*

"The heightened sense of drama and intrigue, combined with a good dose of human interest is what sets Amazing Stories *apart."*
Pamela Klaffke, *Calgary Herald*

"This is popular history as it should be... For this price, buy two and give one to a friend."
Terry Cook, a reader from Ottawa, on **Rebel Women**

"Glasner creates the moment of the explosion itself in graphic detail...she builds detail upon gruesome detail to create a convincingly authentic picture."
Peggy McKinnon, *The Sunday Herald*, on **The Halifax Explosion**

"It was wonderful...I found I could not put it down. I was sorry when it was completed."
Dorothy F. from Manitoba on **Marie-Anne Lagimodière**

"Stories are rich in description, and bristle with a clever, stylish realness."
Mark Weber, *Central Alberta Advisor*, on **Ghost Town Stories II**

"A compelling read. Bertin...has selected only the most intriguing tales, which she narrates with a wealth of detail."
Joyce Glasner, *New Brunswick Reader*, on **Strange Events**

"The resulting book is one readers will want to share with all the women in their lives."
Lynn Martel, *Rocky Mountain Outlook*, on **Women Explorers**

VANCOUVER CANUCKS

AMAZING STORIES

VANCOUVER CANUCKS

Heart-Stopping Stories from
Canada's Most Exciting
Hockey Team

HOCKEY

by Justin Beddall

PUBLISHED BY ALTITUDE PUBLISHING CANADA LTD.
1500 Railway Avenue, Canmore, Alberta T1W 1P6
www.altitudepublishing.com
1-800-957-6888

Extreme care has been taken to ensure that all information presented in
this book is accurate and up to date. Neither the author nor the
publisher can be held responsible for any errors.

Publisher	Stephen Hutchings
Associate Publisher	Kara Turner
Editor	Joan Dixon

We acknowledge the financial support of the Government
of Canada through the Book Publishing Industry Development
Program (BPIDP) for our publishing activities.

Altitude GreenTree Program
Altitude Publishing will plant twice as many trees as were used
in the manufacturing of this product.

National Library of Canada Cataloguing in Publication Data

Beddall, Justin
Vancouver Canucks / Justin Beddall.

(Amazing stories)
Includes bibliographical references.
ISBN 1-55153-792-3

1. Vancouver Canucks (Hockey team)--History.
I. Title. II. Series: Amazing stories (Canmore, Alta.)

GV848.V35B42 2004   796.962'64'0971133   C2004-903748-X

Amazing Stories® is a registered trademark of Altitude Publishing Canada Ltd.

Printed and bound in Canada by Friesens
4 6 8 9 7 5 3

For my father, Michael John Maitland Beddall

Contents

Prologue

Canucks left-winger Geoff Courtnall knew the scouting report on Calgary Flames goaltender Mike Vernon. High, glove side.

The Canucks filed into the visitors' dressing room at the Calgary Saddledome after the third period of game five of the 1994 Stanley Cup playoffs. The players knew if they didn't score a goal in overtime, their season was finished. Courtnall took a few seconds to visualize a goal his former teammate, Wayne Gretzky, had scored against Vernon during the 1988 Stanley Cup playoffs. Shorthanded, Gretzky had skated down the left wing. With Vernon high in the crease to challenge him, he had blasted a slapshot high over the goaltender's glove-hand shoulder.

During the intermission, Courtnall walked out of the dressing room into the corridor where he could light a propane torch to doctor his stick. He put a massive — maybe even illegal — curve on his Easton. If he could get a shot during the overtime period, he was going to shoot high on Vernon.

Eight minutes into the first overtime period, Courtnall got the opportunity he had prepared his stick for. As he hopped over the boards to replace Greg Adams on a line change, Courtnall skated opportunistically down the left wing. A Canucks defenceman broke up a play at the Canucks blueline.

Vancouver Canucks

The puck bounced fortuitously between a Calgary defence-man's legs and onto the streaking Courtnall's stick. Courtnall cruised down towards the Calgary net and wired a slapshot from the top of the face-off circle...

Chapter 1
The Early Years

he spin of a lottery wheel was about to determine the fortunes of the NHL's newest expansion teams — the Vancouver Canucks and the Buffalo Sabres. General manager Bud Poile and the rest of the Canucks' brain trust sat impatiently at a draft table in the Grand Salon room of the swank Queen Elizabeth Hotel in downtown Montreal. Dressed in a dapper black suit, NHL president Clarence Campbell explained the rules of the Amateur and Expansion Drafts. As part of the US$6 million fee to join the National Hockey League for the 1970-71 season, the Canucks and Sabres could each select 18 skaters and 2 goaltenders from the unprotected lists of existing NHL rosters. Perhaps more importantly, one of the teams would also get the opportunity to select the first overall pick

at the NHL's 1970 Amateur Draft.

The lottery wheel was numbered 1 through 13. Campbell flipped a coin to see which general manager would have their first choice of numbers. For each draft, one team would get numbers under seven, the other team, numbers over seven. Buffalo general manager Punch Imlach won the toss and chose the higher numbers for both spins. The white-haired Campbell then stepped up to the red-and-white wheel and gave it a whirl. The room — packed with NHL club officials, newspaper reporters, and fans — fell silent as the wheel made several revolutions before finally stopping. Number eight. The Sabres had won first choice at the NHL Expansion Draft for players that would take place the next day.

The stakes were much higher as Campbell prepared to spin the campy-looking wheel a second time. The top prize: a French-Canadian hockey prodigy named Gilbert Perreault. NHL hockey scouts unanimously agreed that the No. 1 draft choice could provide a successful underpinning for an expansion team for seasons to come.

Like a group of casino gamblers praying for their luck to change, the Vancouver Canucks contingent of management, coaches, and scouts craned their necks with nervous anticipation as Campbell spun the wheel again. Having first choice for the Expansion Draft was good, but first choice in the Amateur Draft would be even better. A hush swept across the noisy room as the wheel began to slow down. "Number 1! Vancouver wins the first choice in the Amateur

Draft!" Campbell announced.

Shouts of victory erupted from the Vancouver Canucks' draft table. They would get the slick forward from the Montreal Junior Canadiens. "We had a great celebration at our table. We were going to get Gilbert Perreault," recalled Canucks public relations director Greg Douglas. "We were all ready to go and dress him up in our jersey. As far as we were concerned, we had him."

But, before the celebratory Canucks brass had a chance to sit down, the destiny of the organization would change dramatically. "Time, Mr. Campbell," Buffalo GM Punch Imlach said calmly. "That's not a one, Mr. Campbell, that's an 11."

"The whole room went quiet," remembered Douglas, who was seated at the Canucks' draft table along with GM Bud Poile, coach Hal Laycoe, and the team's scouting staff. "Everybody looked and realized it was an 11 and our table just went quiet."

Imlach was right. A red-faced Campbell, who had called the number, corrected himself. "Gentlemen, there has been a mistake. The number is 11." Buffalo would win Perreault.

The Canucks would have to settle for the next best player available at the draft: Dale Tallon, a 19-year-old smooth-skating defenceman who could also play forward. Vancouver scout John "Peanuts" O'Flaherty attempted to put a positive spin on the draft-day game of roulette: "Maybe it's just as well, Tallon is a lot tougher than Perreault. Stronger defensively too."

Bud Poile was more candid about the day, which was later dubbed "Black Tuesday" in Canucks hockey lore. "I'm not going to call home tonight. The way things are going, my wife is likely to tell me the house has burned down," he joked half-heartedly.

Before Poile officially made Tallon the first-ever Canucks draft pick, he set about building his team through the Expansion Draft. He'd had much success doing this as the general manager of the expansion Philadelphia Flyers in 1967. After the Sabres selected Tom Webster from the Boston Bruins with the first pick, Poile countered by drafting Boston Bruins defenceman Gary Doak, considered to be the best blueliner left unprotected.

Next, Poile selected Orland Kurtenbach from the New York Rangers. Kurtenbach turned out to be the first gamble that paid off for Vancouver. A 34-year-old Alberta native with a wonky back, Kurtenbach admitted he wasn't surprised to hear his name called out during the Expansion Draft. "I knew I was either going to go to Buffalo or Vancouver. I knew that ahead of time and my preference was Vancouver," he recalled. "I had played for Bud Poile in San Francisco and I played for Punch in Toronto — I guess my only concern was whether my back was going to be OK, which it was. Having played for the old Western League Canucks and then coming back to play for expansion-era Canucks was wonderful." He became the Canucks' first captain.

Poile then selected tough forward Rosaire Paiement,

a player he'd gotten to know while he was general manager of the Flyers. He dipped back into the Flyers' talent pool for a long-haired, 22-year-old goaltender named Dunc Wilson. Like Paiement, Wilson had spent most of his pro career with the Flyers' farm team, the Quebec Aces.

Drafted fourth at the Expansion Draft for his toughness was Pat Quinn, a hardrock 26-year-old defenceman from the Toronto Maple Leafs. Quinn had gained notoriety in the 1968-69 playoffs when he had leveled Boston superstar Bobby Orr. Poile continued to stock his expansion team with character players. He purchased Andre Boudrias from the St. Louis Blues. He also added 37-year-old goaltender Charlie Hodge from the Oakland Seals for some experience between the pipes.

Two months later, on August 5, 1970, the Canucks' No.1 draft pick, Dale Tallon, walked into a press conference inside Vancouver's Devonshire Hotel. Dark-haired, with movie-star good looks, he was decked out in a red jacket, orange floral print shirt, and white slacks. He had just signed the richest deal ever given to an NHL rookie. Scoring 39 goals for the Toronto Marlboros in his last year of junior hockey, Tallon was expected to make an immediate impact on the Canucks blueline. But the Canucks' Douglas wisely observed, "He was a talent but he was young, he wasn't ready. But when you're an expansion team, you make them ready."

Despite losing out on the Gilbert Perreault sweepstakes, Vancouver fans were more than ready for the puck to drop at the Pacific Coliseum. The Vancouver Canucks had finally been granted the right to join the league in 1970-71, after being passed over for an expansion franchise in 1967. While Vancouver hockey fans rejoiced at the news, no local businessmen had come forward to put up the franchise fee necessary to secure a team. The search for an owner eventually led to Minnesota businessman Thomas Scallen and his partner Lyman Walters. In 1969, Scallen purchased the Western Hockey League (WHL) Vancouver Canucks to bring into the NHL. As owners of the Medical Investment Corporation, Scallen and Walters knew a lot about running a multimillion-dollar business, but they knew very little about hockey.

Following a cocktail reception at the swanky Bayshore Inn, Walters admitted he wasn't even crazy about the team's moniker. In *The Vancouver Canucks Story*, author Denny Boyd reported him saying, "The word Canuck strikes me as a slang expression that I don't particularly like. If there are no serious objections from the fans, we are going to consider a name change." Fortunately, when Walters and Scallen learned that the team name was in homage to Johnny Canuck — the Canadian fighting man — they reconsidered their position.

Although Vancouver had been snubbed for the six-team expansion in the first go-round, the city had already experienced a rich hockey history — and a Stanley Cup. In 1915, the Vancouver Millionaires finished in first place in the fledgling Pacific Coast Hockey Association, an upstart league formed by future Hall-of-Famers Lester and Frank Patrick. The team's first-place finish meant they would face the Ottawa Senators, the champion of the more established NHL, in a best-of-five championship. The Millionaires were considered one of the best hockey teams ever assembled. Led by Fred "Cyclone" Taylor, they swept the Sens before packed crowds in the 10,500-seat Denman Arena on the shores of Coal Harbour. They outscored their eastern foes 26-8.

More than half a century later, Vancouver hockey fans were eager for a return visit from Lord Stanley's cup. While the rookie American owners of the Canucks had a dearth of hockey experience, they had the common sense to hire a veteran hockey man to run the franchise. Poile had played six seasons in the NHL before becoming a player-coach in 1950-51 for Tulsa in the United States Hockey League. Two years later, he became coach of the WHL's Edmonton Flyers. When Vancouverite Coley Hall purchased San Francisco's team in the WHL, he hired Poile as coach and general manager. Poile won WHL titles in 1964 and 1965. When Philadelphia was granted an expansion NHL franchise in 1967, Poile was named general manager. Poile's hockey smarts became even more evident when the Flyers captured the Western Division in just their first season on Broad Street.

The 45-year-old Poile's search for the Canucks' first coach landed on Hal Laycoe, who had been the coach for the Los Angeles Kings the season prior, compiling a 5-18-1 record. His NHL coaching resume only included 24 games, but he had an impressive record as coach of the WHL's

Portland Buckaroos, winning seven titles in nine seasons, including a pair of Lester Patrick championships.

As Poile continued to cobble together his fledgling hockey organization, Vancouver's chief nemesis, Punch Imlach, would strike again. Not only had the Buffalo GM largely determined which players would play in Vancouver, he also influenced the uniforms they played in. Poile wanted his team colours to be blue and gold, but Punch had filed his selection for the same combination with NHL headquarters before Poile. As a result, the team had to settle on royal blue, kelly green, and white — symbolic of the ocean, forest, and snow-capped mountains in British Columbia. Local artist Joe Borovich designed the first uniform logo: a stylized "C" in the shape of a hockey rink with a white stick in the middle.

The uniform, name, and management structure in place, the expansion Canucks walked out of the tunnel from the dressing room on October 9, 1970. Their first-ever game at the Pacific Coliseum against the Los Angeles Kings was not sold out only because of a glitch in the team's ticket system. An epic pre-game ceremony included such dignitaries as NHL president Clarence Campbell, Premier W.A.C. Bennett, Native Chief Dan George, and Cyclone Taylor. In a full-length fur coat, Vancouver mayor Tom Campbell waved to the crowd.

After the Kings got out to a 2-0 lead, defenceman Barry Wilkins doubled his career goal totals with a backhander that got past the Kings goalie. He instantly made himself a piece of Canucks hockey history. Still, despite all the hype, the first game was less than memorable.

"There was a very long pre-game ceremony, and they introduced everyone in the building. And when the game finally started it was not a good hockey game, it was dull ... much more memorable was the next game," long-time Canucks broadcaster Jim Robson recalled. Two nights later, thanks to a pair of goals from left-winger Wayne Maki, the Canucks defeated the Toronto Maple Leafs 5-3. This time, in front of a sell-out crowd of 15,542, they recorded their first NHL win against one of the most storied franchises in hockey.

The Canucks went on to win more games that year than any of the 653,898 fans who bought tickets could have ever imagined. They finished with a record of 24-46-8, which slotted them in sixth spot in the East Division. "That first-year team was not a bad team," said Robson. Had it not been for a season-ending knee injury to captain Kurtenbach, the team might have even challenged for a playoff berth.

Despite the pressure heaped on his shoulders by the press and local hockey fandom, Dale Tallon had an impressive rookie season. He scored 14 goals and added 42 assists, breaking Bobby Orr's rookie record. Andre "Super Pest" Boudrias led the team with 25 goals and 41 assists. Paiement surprised NHL onlookers with 34 goals and 62 points, along with 152 penalty minutes. Indeed, it was a breakthrough year for "Crackling Rosie" Paiement, who had scored just four goals and five assists in his previous 43 NHL games. In all, four Canucks forwards finished with more than 20 goals each, for the first time in their careers.

Kurtenbach, the team's MVP, recalled the year with pleasure: "It was wonderful for a lot of other players that had been with other NHL clubs and now had the opportunity to play a lot of hockey ... One of the fusing points was we had some vets and they were good people ... Gary Doak, Pat Quinn, Charlie Hodge ... There were a lot of colourful guys."

And there were several colourful moments in that first season. As Boyd related in his book, Buffalo's Imlach had hurled another bomb at his expansion cousin before their first encounter. He referred to the Canucks as the "The 4-F club — Feeble, Folding, Fumbling, and Frustrated." General manager Bud Poile could only bite all his pencils in half while trying to think of an appropriate comeback. In "the closest thing to a religious experience that Poile ever had in hockey," Paiement scored four goals as the Canucks defeated the Sabres 6-3.

On November 5, the Canucks won their first road game against Buffalo. The night witnessed Vancouver netminder Dunc Wilson stopping the team's first penalty shot against Sabres forward Paul Andrea.

Broadcaster Jim Robson, who called all 78 games that season, has a particular favourite moment: "The highlight without question was the February 16 game when they beat the Boston Bruins. Boston were the Stanley Cup champions and they had Cheevers in goal and they had Orr ... and Esposito, Hodge and Cashman, Sanderson ... they had a powerhouse and the Canucks beat them 5-4. Rosaire Paiement scored his third goal of the night with something like 56 seconds left...breaking a 4-4 tie. It was a fantastic game and the place went nuts. That was the most memorable game in the first season."

The first season also provided some follies. George Gardner, nicknamed the "Roly-poly Goalie" because of his steadfast lack of conditioning, let in a soft goal during a Sunday game at Madison Square Garden. Ranger Vic Hatfield had golfed a shot and scored from centre ice. Nobody could figure out how it happened. As it turned out, Gardner, an avid gambler, was busy concentrating on something else. He was squinting at the read-o-graph that displayed updated NFL games results at the opposite end of the arena. Douglas explained, "He had a ton of money on the game and he was watching to see how San Diego was doing and didn't even see the puck go in."

The Canucks had a difficult time living up to the high standards set in their inaugural season. Despite continued goal production from Boudrias and Kurtenbach, the Canucks finished the next season with 48 points. Paiement, meanwhile, struggled, scoring just 10 goals. The big forward's 37-game slump prompted the team to invite world-famous hypnotist "The Amazing Raveen" to help end the goal drought. Raveen attended the Canucks' weekly Tuesday luncheon and hypnotized Paiement, telling him, "You will score tonight."

"It didn't work," Douglas recalled. The team's record was a harbinger of things to come. The next season (1972-73), the Vancouver Canucks' losing ways continued. They finished with a record of 22-47-9, seventh in the East Division. Shortly afterwards, Bud Poile suffered a heart attack and was forced to resign. Hal Laycoe, who had been kicked upstairs as vice-president, was brought on as interim GM. Behind the scenes, a power struggle for the team continued between minority shareholder Coley Hall and owner Tom Scallen. Hall usurped control of the team. He was largely responsible for the hiring of new coach Bill McCreary. He also orchestrated the May 14 trade that sent Dale Tallon to the Chicago Blackhawks.

In addition to scoring 44 goals and 93 assists in 222 games as an original Canuck, Tallon also provided some dubious highlights off the ice. Boyd recalled one: "Dale Tallon, the glamour-dripping super-rookie of the first NHL season, is a young man of many means, a potentially great defenceman, a top golfer, a member of the NHL's best-dressed team and a two-country lady killer. He is also a totally unpredictable radio interviewee. Once a radioman asked Tallon what his relaxing plans were for a brief Canuck layoff and Tallon answered, 'Wall to wall broads.'"

In exchange for their star draft pick, Vancouver received defenceman Jerry Korab and flamboyant goaltender Gary Smith. "Suitcase" Smith was a curly-haired free spirit who had shared the Vezina trophy with Tony Esposito in 1971-72.

Suitcase, with his penchant for full-length fur coats and all-star quips, would become an immediate hit in Vancouver. "Everything you've heard about me is absolutely true ... I am a tremendous goalie," he told reporters after arriving in Vancouver. "He was a character ... Smitty one night let in an overtime goal and stormed off the ice and down the chute and went straight to his car and drove home in his equipment," recalled Douglas.

During the 1973-74 season, Suitcase carried the team. He played in 65 games, compiling a 20-33-8 record and a 3.44 goals-against average. But not even the six-foot-four Smith could stop the team's struggles on and off the ice.

"You could not get a ticket at the Pacific Coliseum for the first two and a half years. The fans were satisfied with what they were seeing except our team was not winning," recalled Douglas. "Midway through the third year, the novelty had worn off and that's when the players began to feel the pressure. That's when management felt the pressure."

In January, Phil Maloney replaced Bill McCreary behind the bench and the team finished with a pitiable 59 points. That summer, Scallen was forced to sell the team after being found guilty in a B.C. provincial court. He had illegally converted $3 million of the money raised from investors in the hockey team to pay off his own personal business debt and created a false stock prospectus. Television and radio magnate Frank Griffiths's Western Broadcasting Company bought the team for $9 million. In 1974-75, Griffiths's Canucks won the Smythe Division championship. Fans at the Pacific Coliseum finally had something to cheer about.

Chapter 2
Tiger and the Cup

ave "Tiger" Williams arrived at the Vancouver International Airport sporting a white cowboy hat, a hunting vest, and jeans. He brought with him a penalty-minute rap sheet a mile long — and a fierce determination to win. "He typifies what we're looking for, the guy who will do anything to win. Maybe the guys we are getting aren't as talented as the two we gave up but their work habits are a lot better," said coach Harry Neale.

The February 18, 1980, trade that made the 26-year-old Williams a Canuck was a risky move. Vancouver Canucks general manager Jake Milford traded talented but under-achieving first-round draft picks Rick Vaive and Bill Derlago for Williams and checking forward Jerry Butler. On paper, the trade tilted heavily in favour of the Leafs. As Williams later proved, hockey isn't played on a sheet of loose-leaf.

Williams had spent the first five and a half seasons of his NHL career in Toronto. Mostly he rode shotgun on the Leafs' top line with Darryl Sittler and Lanny McDonald. Milford believed Williams's fierce competitiveness would rub off on the bottom-dwelling Canucks franchise. In his first full season with the Canucks (1980-81), the 180-pound left-winger earned 343 penalty minutes but scored a career-high 35 goals. It earned him a trip to the NHL all-star game. His penchant for gooning it up and his flamboyant goal-scoring celebration — "the Tiger Shuffle" — immediately endeared him to Canucks fans. But more importantly, the arrival of the gritty Saskatchewan native shook up the country-club atmosphere that had infected the Canucks' dressing room. "Any good athlete always thinks that you're a day away from making the difference," Williams said. "If you don't think that, you should probably be a welder."

Although Williams's offense tailed off in 1981-82 when he scored just 17 times, No. 22 was the instigator of an incident that would launch the Canucks on their improbable 1982 Stanley Cup run. The cinematic moment was reminiscent of the 1970s cult classic *Slap Shot*. At Le Colisée in Quebec City on March 20, Williams took a run at the Nordiques' star centre, Peter Stastny. During an ensuing melee, a fan reached over the boards and took a swing at Williams. Coach Harry Neale and several of Williams's teammates vaulted

Tiger Williams

themselves into the stands in pursuit of the overzealous fan.

Defending the most penalized player in the NHL cost Neale a 10-game suspension: the final five games in the regular season, along with the first five in the play-offs. Defenceman Doug Halward received a seven-game suspension for his part in the altercation. Still, as Williams later recounted in his book, *Tiger: A Hockey Story,* "An incident like that unifies a team dramatically."

With Neale's banishment to the press box, Roger Neilson stepped behind the bench. The 47-year-old had been hired as Neale's associate coach by Jake Milford the previous summer. Williams had played for Neilson in Toronto where Neilson had established a reputation as a tireless tactician and a pioneer in the use of video analysis. "Because I'd worked with Roger Neilson before, it was no great surprise to me that he could organize so well, hand down game plans that were like a set of military instructions. For the other guys, it was a revelation," Williams said, "and they responded tremendously."

For some players on the team, like high-scoring winger Darcy Rota, Neilson brought a fresh approach to the rink. "He always made practices very interesting. He was a great innovator."

As the rookie head coach of the Toronto Maple Leafs in 1977-78, Neilson had proven himself a master strategist and motivator. He led the Leafs past the Los Angeles Kings and the highly favoured New York Islanders in the playoffs. Could he have similar success in Vancouver? During the final five games of the regular season under Neilson, the Canucks went undefeated, forging a 4-0-1 record. They hammered the Los Angeles Kings 7-4 in the final game of the regular season to finish with 77 points, second in the Smythe Division.

For the first time in franchise history, the Canucks had

home-ice advantage for the opening round of the Stanley Cup playoffs. More importantly, the team was on a roll, having finished the season with six wins and three ties. "The incident in Quebec was part of it, but when I look at the last nine games, we went into the playoffs on a real high even though we finished the year under .500," Rota recalled. "For me that was a real key factor: we went into the playoffs believing we could beat anybody."

The Canucks had every reason to feel confident. During the regular season, the team was fifth best in the league in goals-against. Leading the team from the blueline was captain Kevin McCarthy, Lars Lindgren, Colin Campbell, and a big, stay-at-home defenceman, Harold Snepsts. In goal was an unheralded French Canadian, Richard Brodeur, acquired from the Islanders in 1980. He played in 52 regular-season games with the Canucks, compiling a regular-season record of 20-18-2 and 3.35 goals-against average.

At the same time, the team scored a franchise-high 290 goals. Gritty wingers Stan Smyl, Curt Fraser, and Darcy Rota combined for 82 goals. They complemented a talented centre-ice corps that included Thomas Gradin, Ivan Hlinka, and Ivan Boldirev. "We had some skill guys, particularly down the middle but mostly there were a lot of gritty, hardworking competitive guys that were willing to pay the price," recalled Rota. "We were a very focused team that played very hard."

The Canucks lineup at this time included five Swedes: Gradin, Lars Molin, Lars Lindgren, Per-Olov Brasar, and

Anders Elderbrink. Some questioned if they could handle the rigors of the second season, but Tiger Williams wasn't about to let his teammates be intimidated. "He would have little meetings with [the] Swedes and he was telling them that he would look after them and not to worry about anything, just go in and play hard and they would be looked after," *Province* reporter Tony Gallagher recalled.

Unfortunately, two days before hosting its first-ever series opener against the Calgary Flames, a pall fell over the club. As the team scrimmaged during an optional skate at East Van's Britannia Ice Rink, Kevin McCarthy got tangled up with forward Curt Fraser. The team's captain fell awkwardly, breaking his ankle. "That was really quite devastating. Kevin was a great team guy, a great leader," said Rota. Not only had the Canucks lost a valuable member of their power play, they were already threadbare on the blueline. Doug Halward was still serving the last two games of his suspension for the famous brawl in Quebec. So the Canucks were left with Snepsts, Campbell, and Lindgren as the only veterans on a defense corps that included little-known rookies Neil Belland and Andy Schliebener.

Tiger Williams seemed unfazed by the loss of McCarthy. "We'll beat them," Williams predicted prior to the series opener. Williams's blunt comments were prophetic — literally and figuratively. Game one at the Pacific Coliseum was only eight seconds old when acting captain Stan Smyl gave the Canucks a 1-0 lead on a pass from linemate Thomas Gradin.

On the ensuing face-off, Calgary penalty-minute leader Willi Plett tried to shift the momentum of the game by picking a fight with Curt Fraser. Fraser was considered by many to be the best pound-for-pound scrapper on the Canucks team. He knocked Plett to the ice with an overhand right — to the delight of 11,701 Pacific Coliseum fans. "That set the series," Williams said. The Canucks won the game 5-3.

In order to douse the Flames, Roger Neilson had devised a game plan to shut down Lanny McDonald. McDonald had scored 34 goals for Calgary in 55 games after being acquired from the Colorado Rockies earlier in the season. Every time the mustached sniper set foot on the ice, Neilson countered with Williams, who stuck to his old linemate like an offensive-sucking leach. "It's a job," said Williams about his checking assignment at the time. "We knew how important Lanny is to the team and we have to contain him." Later, Williams admitted that the series strained the pair's off-ice friendship. Williams elbowed, kneed, slashed, and agitated McDonald, oftentimes goading him into the penalty box. McDonald didn't register a goal in the series.

In game two in overtime, Williams was the one being cross-checked to the ice by Flames defenceman Bob Murdoch. Parking himself in front of the net, Tiger nevertheless backhanded a pass from Lars Molin past Calgary goalie Pat Riggin. The goal gave the Canucks a 2-1 win. "It wasn't pretty but it went in," Williams told reporters. In game three, Williams also scored the game-winner at 8:17 of the third period.

Vancouver went on to a 3-1 win, sweeping the Flames. When they beat Calgary, as Tiger had predicted, they started to believe in themselves even more.

Tiger tales began making the front pages of the sports sections. "I've long suspected that The Tiger ultimately was destined for heroics — sometime, some place, and with some previously unsung team which needed only the inspirational spark of one man's performance to lift that team from mediocrity to success," wrote columnist Jim Coleman.

Vancouver players knew there was more to their win than Tiger. Their stubby beer-bottle-shaped goaltender had almost single-handedly limited the high-scoring Flames to just five goals in three games. He stopped 103 of the 108 shots he faced. Following the series victory, King Richard's teammates were already comparing him to the Great One. "You talk about Richard the same way you talk about Gretzky," Thomas Gradin said.

The team's unofficial theme song, "Freeze Frame" by the J. Giels Band, blared in the Canucks locker room, in celebration of the franchise's first-ever playoff series victory. Meanwhile, the Los Angeles Kings were also celebrating. They had finished the regular season a whopping 48 points behind Wayne Gretzky's Oilers. The underdog Kings came back from a 5-1 deficit in the third period to defeat Edmonton 6-5 in overtime in what was called "the Miracle on Manchester." They took a 2-1 series lead over the Oilers. The Oilers won game four 3-2. In a fifth, and deciding, game in Edmonton,

34

Los Angeles completed the improbable upset with a 7-4 win.

Instead of starting on the road against the Oilers, the Canucks were able to pull out the welcome mat at the Pacific Coliseum for the Kings. Gallagher commented, "Let's be reasonable here; they probably wouldn't have beaten the Oilers. That was the biggest break."

The Kings boasted the potent "Triple Crown" line of 50-goal scorer Marcel Dionne and wingmen Dave Taylor and Charlie Simmer. But the Canucks had a new ice-field battle plan prepared by their hot general behind the bench. In game one, Czech import Ivan Hlinka scored a pair of goals. Centre Gary Lupul, a native of Powell River, added the game-winner at the five-minute mark of the third period, giving the Canucks a 3-2 victory. The victory extended the Canucks' unbeaten streak under Neilson to nine games.

But the Triple Crown line, held in check in the first game, got on the score sheet during game two. After Rota opened the scoring with his first of the series, Taylor and Dionne replied. B.C.-born Kings sniper Steve Bozek scored in 4:33 of overtime to give the Kings a 3-2 victory.

Although his suspension had expired, Neale wisely left Neilson in command of the team. The Canucks took a series lead two nights later at the Great Western Forum — thanks to an unlikely goal outburst from Colin Campbell. He netted the game's first goal at 18:09 of the first, and the game-winner 1:23 into overtime. "We usually tell Collie to shoot the puck into the corner," Neilson joked after the game. "He doesn't even score in practice." Brodeur, meanwhile, earned himself another game-star selection, stopping 41 of 44 shots.

In game four, the Canucks scored a 5-4 win. A three-goal outburst from Fraser, Williams, and Rota in the second period chased Kings goaltender Mario Lessard from the net. The Canucks had a 3-1 series lead — despite being outshot 116-67. The diminutive Brodeur cast a very large shadow from his goal crease. "Every time they're down, he comes up with a big save and gives them a lift," Kings sniper Marcel Dionne complained prior to game five.

After rookie Kings centre Bernie Nicholls hushed another sellout crowd just 90 seconds into game five, the Canucks came back for a 5-2 victory. They won the Smythe Division championship, thanks to a pair of second-period goals by Prince George native Rota. In the dying seconds of the game, jubilant fans serenaded the Kings home, with "Na Na Hey Hey Goodbye." The song became a playoff tradition at the Pacific Coliseum that spring.

The Campbell Conference final was against the Chicago Blackhawks, a team led by 119-point centre Denis Savard and Norris Trophy-candidate defenceman Doug Wilson. Game one turned out to be a long night for the upstart Vancouver Canucks. Tied 1-1 after three periods, forward Jim Nill finally scored at 8:58 of the second overtime period. It was the longest playoff game in Canucks history: 88 minutes and 58 seconds. The Canucks again stole the game, thanks to the puck-stopping magic of goaltender Brodeur. "Preceding the winner was the most incredible goaltending one can hope to see from a stubby French-Canadian who remains almost insanely cool under duress," wrote Gallagher. "Brodeur stopped at least eight scoring chances in overtime alone and heaven knows how many before that."

NHL teams scouting the Canucks seemed confounded by Brodeur's style. Gallagher recalled a conversation with Neil Smith, who was, at the time, a scout with the New York Islanders. "He would say they couldn't get a book on Brodeur at all because they would watch him during the warm-up and he would never stop a single puck. And then during the game he never gave up anything, so they never really knew how he was beaten or where his weaknesses were, because the puck was always stopped."

The 18,610 fans who packed noisy Chicago Stadium for game two would witness one of the most memorable moments in Vancouver Canucks history. The Hawks led 2-0 after two periods, but Stan Smyl scored just over a minute into the third to spark the Canucks bench. The lift, however, was short-lived. Denis Savard restored Chicago's two-goal lead at 4:42. When an apparent Canucks goal by Curt Fraser was disallowed, Roger Neilson began to seethe with anger over the inconsistent officiating that seemed to favour the home team. Savard scored again on Chicago's ninth power-play advantage, making the score 4-1 in a fight-marred game. By the third period, Neilson couldn't hide his contempt towards referee Bob Meyers. Standing beside him, Tiger Williams suggested, "Let's throw the sticks on the ice."

"No," Neilson responded, "we're going to surrender."

Neilson put a white towel on the end of a hockey stick in mock surrender. At 16:23 of the third period, Neilson was ejected from the game. Williams and Gerry Minor, both of whom followed their coach with the towel-waving gesture, received 10-minute misconduct penalties. Referee Meyers had penalized Vancouver 23 times for 101 minutes — 19 more PIMs than the Hawks.

With his actions, Neilson had turned a disheartening loss into an emotional rallying point for the Canucks. After the game, defenceman Colin Campbell said, "Roger didn't lose his head. When he does something like that, there's a useful purpose to it."

Darcy Rota agreed. "We weren't going to win the game ... we came back to Vancouver and even ... the truck to meet us had white towels, it was unbelievable. And we came out to a sea of towels in game three; that to me was a real pivotal point of the playoff run."

Before game three, entrepreneurs ringed the Pacific Coliseum with towels the size of face cloths. They were now emblazoned with the slogan "Take no prisoners" and sold for five bucks. Canucks fans quickly adopted the new rallying cry.

The NHL head office was far less amused by Neilson's ref-baiting antics, and fined the team $10,000. Neilson himself received a $1000 penalty for his indiscretion behind the bench. NHL official Brian O'Neill said it "disgraced the championship series. Actions that demean our officials will not be tolerated."

Neilson's towel-waving tactic, however, may have affected the officiating. During game three, the Canucks' checking line of Williams, Gerry Minor, and Lars Molin manhandled Savard all night. They frustrated both the NHL's sixth-leading scorer and Chicago coach Bob Pulford. "It's pretty hard to play hockey when you're carrying them on your back all night," a disgusted Pulford seethed. "How they let all that go on Savard is beyond me. Maybe those white flags worked." Fans had plenty of reasons to wave the towels. Stan Smyl scored the game-winner at 2:05 of the third.

Meanwhile, Conn Smythe trophy candidate Richard Brodeur was gaining a regal following in Vancouver, inspiring bumper stickers, towels, and buttons. A group called King Richard's Army even recorded a single in his honour, called "King Richard." Teammate Williams seemed to be equally impressed with Brodeur: "He's a cool little frog. He is a professional right through. I haven't met anybody in the game I respect more."

Brodeur frustrated the Hawks again in game four. Boldirev scored a pair in a 5-3 victory that sent the Canucks back to Chicago. They were on the verge of clinching their first-ever trip to the Stanley Cup final.

Game one's double-overtime hero, Jim Nill, opened the scoring just 2:40 into game five. Stan Smyl added his sixth goal of the playoffs just over a minute later, giving the Canucks an early 2-0 lead over Tony Esposito and the Hawks. The fight-filled first period included Ron Delorme's drubbing of Grant Mulvey. Then, after Mulvey scored early in the third period to make it 3-2, the Canucks answered with three goals to make the final score 6-2. For Rota, who had suited up with the Hawks for six seasons, the victory tasted especially sweet. "To win game five in Chicago Stadium and I scored the fifth goal, that was the biggest game ever. For the first time in our team history we went to the Stanley Cup final."

Not even Canucks management had planned for a trip to the Stanley Cup final.

"That team had a lot of hurdles," recalled broadcaster Jim Robson. "They had to go right from Chicago to New York and the Canucks, not planning to get to the final, hadn't made any hotel arrangements and we stayed at a hotel that was miles away from the rink in Long Island."

The Canucks now faced the two-time defending Stanley Cup champions, the New York Islanders. Led by Mike Bossy, Brian Trottier, John Tonelli, Bill Nystrom, Denis Potvin, and goalie Billy Smith, the Islanders had finished the season atop the Patrick Division with an enviable 54-16-10 record.

And despite the Vancouver Canucks' miraculous playoff run, the New York press showed little respect for the team from the West Coast. They ridiculed the Canucks' road jerseys, calling them "Darth Vadar costumes, with jagged, garish, orange and yellow stripes — probably the ugliest uniforms in professional sports." They also accused the Canucks of playing a vapid brand of hockey. *New York Times* reporter George Vecsey wrote, "Neilson's Canucks have exploited the gap in the rules." The Islanders' general manager, Bill Torrey, told the same reporter, "It's like a rugby match, anything is possible. It's the way Roger teaches. You know that when you play his team, the game is going to be dragged down."

The Canucks weren't about to be dragged down by the New York press. In game one, centreman Thomas Gradin opened the scoring just 1:29 into the first period. The Canucks found themselves tied 5-5 with the mighty Isles heading into yet another sudden-death overtime. Unfortunately, with just two seconds remaining in the first overtime period, defence-man Harold Snepsts's errant pass deep in the Vancouver end was picked off by Mike Bossy. He wristed a 20-footer into the top left corner of the net, past a helpless and surprised Richard Brodeur.

After the game, the quixotic Williams — his body bruised and battered from the playoff run — remained upbeat about the Canucks' chances: "We'll win our three home games. That means we'll just have to win one here." At home, Canucks fandom remained optimistic too. Some waited more than 40 hours in line for tickets to Thursday's game three in Vancouver. Nearly 50 fans couldn't wait to see the Canucks' on-ice debut in the Stanley Cup final and paid $870 to fly to Uniondale with a tour group. In game two, they watched their Canucks play valiantly again, leading 3-2 heading into the third period. But the Islander machine kicked into high gear, scoring four third-period tallies for a 6-4 win.

Williams was right, the Canucks would need to win all their home games. By the time the Canucks had touched down at Vancouver International Airport, "Towel Power" had officially captivated the province. Tourism British Columbia officials culled signatures from the premier and members of the legislature on a 300-metre long towel to hang inside the Coliseum for game three. The towels, however, would be used to mop up the tears of the suddenly downcast Canucks fans when the Islanders scored a convincing 3-0 victory. On paper, and on the ice, the Islanders proved to be a much better hockey team. "I don't think anybody in the world would have beaten them tonight," Williams said after the game.

In game four, after Butch Goring opened the scoring at 11:38 of the first period, Vancouver fans finally had something to cheer about. Stan Smyl scored his ninth goal of the playoffs to even the score at 1-1. However, Mike Bossy scored his 16th and 17th goals of the playoffs on power plays in the second. The Islanders skated off with the Stanley Cup. Williams, who had clashed with the stick-swinging Isles goaltender throughout the four-game series, still just shrugged his shoulders after the game. "I would have bet my house that they wouldn't have beaten us four straight." He had tried his hardest, finishing the playoffs with 10 points and a Canuck-record 116 penalty minutes.

Williams suited up in two more playoff series for the

Canucks, in 1982-83 and 1983-84, but the team didn't advance past the first round. "They called it a bad trade after Vaive scored 50," said Robson. But Harry Neale had no regrets about the deal. "He would always say 'What do you mean? We got to the final with Tiger Williams, [Toronto] never got to the final.'"

Chapter 3
Pavel Bure:
Rocket Launch

he covert Moscow hockey insider who tipped off the Vancouver Canucks about Pavel Bure remains a shadowy figure to this day. "Only three people know his name," Brian Burke (at the time Canucks VP) confided to the *New York Times*. "Pat Quinn, [scout] Mike Penny and myself." The information the Muscovite passed along to the Canucks sparked a cold war at the 1989 NHL Entry Draft in Minnesota.

Had Communism fallen a couple years earlier, Pavel Bure would have been an obvious first-round pick at the draft. The 18-year-old rookie of the year had scored 17 goals in just 32 games in the Soviet elite league in 1988-89. He was arguably the most talented player available in the draft but the climate in the Soviet Union at the time made it difficult to bring players to North America unless they defected. All 21 NHL teams were unwilling to gamble an early round pick on the talented Russian. And after the third round, European players who hadn't played at least 11 games at their country's elite level for two seasons were not eligible for the draft.

According to information circulated to NHL teams, Bure had only suited up for five games with the Central Red Army during the 1987-88 season, meaning he wasn't eligible after the third round. The Canucks had better information, said Burke. "Our man in Moscow kept telling us Pasha, which is what everyone in Russia there called him, had played 11 league games and two scheduled international exhibition games." Vancouver was going to take him in the eighth round until they found out Edmonton had the same plan, so they took him in the sixth.

After NHL vice-president Brian O'Neill announced that the Canucks had selected Pavel Bure of the Soviet Union with the 113th pick, a storm of disapproval erupted. The general managers and hockey scouts huddled at draft tables inside the Metropolitan Sports Center in Bloomington. Several clubs protested the pick. "They were tossing expletives at me and everybody else on the Canucks," Burke said. "Because of the controversy, the NHL had to conduct an investigation."

The Canucks were delighted to have stolen Bure at the draft, but the nagging question remained: Would the pick hold up? They awaited NHL president John Ziegler's ruling on Bure's draft eligibility. With Bure, the Canucks could ice a legitimate game breaker in the lineup — for the first time in the franchise's dismal history.

Playing on a line with Alexander Mogilny and Sergei Fedorov at the 1989 World Junior Championship (WJC), Bure had scored seven goals and three assists in seven games. He earned honours as the best forward at the tournament. But Bure's future in Vancouver seemed unlikely. Nearly a year after the draft, Ziegler ruled against the Canucks, making Bure eligible for selection in the 1990 Entry Draft. Not easily dissuaded, the Canucks enlisted the help of veteran superstar Igor Larionov, who had signed with the Canucks in 1989. Using his Moscow connections, he was able to cull Central Red Army game summary sheets that proved Bure had played the required number of games to be eligible for the draft — just as the Moscow informant had said. After reviewing the information obtained by the Canucks, Ziegler reversed his decision on the eve of the 1990 draft. Burke said the Canucks had been confident their pick would stand. "This informant in Russia got copies of the game sheets that he played in and there were two exhibition games that Bure played in against league opponents that counted. I think Mr. Ziegler made the right decision based on the evidence."

Vancouver still had to get Bure into a Canucks uniform. His linemates at the WJC — left-winger Alexander Mogilny and centre Sergei Fedorov — had already defected from the USSR to start their NHL careers. Red Army officials weren't keen on seeing the final third depart. The three youngsters had been expected to replace the famous, but aging, KLM line — Vladimir Krutov, Igor Larionov, and Sergei Makarov. But Bure, who'd already completed his mandatory two-year military service, balked at re-signing with the Red Army. Many believe he was left off the Soviet roster for the 1991 Canada Cup as a punishment for this perceived insubordination. The snub likely hastened Bure's decision. With help from a Russian living in California, he flew to the U.S. in September 1991, with father Vladimir, a former Olympic swimmer, and brother Valeri.

In his first interview through a translator, Pavel predicted he would score a lot in the NHL. "He was confident he would score 50 goals ... and that's one of the reasons there was this enormous build up to him," recalled sportswriter Tony Gallagher. Canucks players had the chance to meet their potential new teammate after an early season game in California. Few of them could believe Bure would have an immediate impact. "After the [San Jose] game he came into the room and shakes everyone's hand and I remember we were all thinking, 'This is the guy everyone keeps talking about and he looks like a little school boy. This kid can't weigh more than 50 pounds soaking wet,'" recalled defenceman Jyrki Lumme.

Nonetheless, in October 1991, 20-year-old Bure signed a four-year deal worth US$2.7 million. The Central Red Army protested that Bure was still under contract until after the 1992 Olympic Games in Albertville, France. The two clubs faced off in a U.S. courtroom. The Canucks offered to pay the Russian team $200,000 compensation. The Soviets balked at the offer, demanding $250,000. Anxious to start his NHL career, Bure broke the stalemate himself. He stood up and said he'd pay the difference. Out of the side of his mouth, Burke told him to sit down and shut up. "But he's like, 'No, I want to play in the NHL. If I have to, I'll pay.' He was willing to take $50,000 out of his signing bonus to play," recalled Burke.

The next day, Burke met Bure at the Canadian embassy in Seattle to get his work visa. Wanting to avoid a media crush at the Vancouver airport, Burke made alternate travel plans to get Bure from Washington State to the Pacific Coliseum. "I rented a car and drove him across. He was working on his English the whole drive up, 'What's that?' [he would ask] ... That's a river ..."

Bure's much-anticipated debut with the Canucks was against the Winnipeg Jets less than a week later. On his first shift, wearing No. 10, he accelerated into a whitish blur over the Jets' blueline and gave long-suffering Canucks fans their first real out-of-seat hockey experience. "That might be the most memorable night in the history of the Canucks, his first game," recalled Gallagher. "I would say that really stands out to me as maybe the most fun evening of all time with the Canucks ... from that time forward, every time [Bure] touched the puck, everyone was just incredibly excited."

Although the balletic Russian was kept off the score

sheet, he managed three scoring chances, including a third-period breakaway. He gave every one of the 16,123 at the sold-out Pacific Coliseum reason to believe they had witnessed the debut of a superstar-in-the-making.

Sportswriters struggled to find the superlatives to describe the awesome speed and puck-handling ability of the young Soviet star. "Like a football player taking receipt of a punt at his own goal line, Pavel Bure, the Red Rocket, took off like a lightning bolt, side-stepped a couple of defenders, zoomed past another who mistook him for an X-ray, then darted for the opposing goal," wrote *Vancouver Sun* sports reporter Mike Beamish.

Even Bure's teammates stood up at the bench and watched with amazement as Bure rushed the puck. "In his first game, even guys on the bench, we're going, 'Wow! What a great player!' He's definitely one of the most exciting players I've ever played with. Sometimes you see some guys that can skate like the wind but they can't carry a puck in their pocket but Pavel could handle the puck pretty good and he was a great passer too," recalled Lumme.

Vancouver Sun hockey beat reporter Iain MacIntyre would be largely responsible for creating an appropriate sobriquet for the young Russian. He wrote, "If Winnipeg are the Jets, then what do you call Pavel Bure? How about the Russian Rocket? OK, so maybe some football player named Raghib calls himself that, but it fits Bure perfectly. He is the fastest Soviet creation since Sputnik." The moniker stuck.

Pavel Bure

After the game, the angelic-faced Bure said through an interpreter, "I will remember everything about this night for the rest of my life. Thank you to everybody, the fans, my teammates, and coaches. It was my fault I didn't score." For a reporter like Gallagher, who had been forced to sit in the press box through successive seasons of Canucks hockey mediocrity, Bure was a salvation. "Hip, hip, Bure," he gushed, following the Jets game.

Bure wouldn't need to do much apologizing about his inability to score that season. Vancouver's gift from the hockey gods managed to score 34 goals and 60 points. He earned a Calder Trophy as the NHL's top rookie, appearing in only 65 games.

Igor Larinov, who had joined the Canucks along with Valdimir Krutov in 1989, helped his comrade adapt to the rigors of the NHL and acclimatize to North American culture. New best friend Gino Odjick helped Bure to learn English and to play cards. Bure also proved as a rookie that his rocket-fuelled rushes wouldn't be aborted during the tighter-checking playoffs. In his first post-season, Bure registered six goals and four assists in 13 games, including his first NHL hat trick against the Winnipeg Jets in game six of the opening round.

In his first full season with the Canucks, Bure bettered his own predictions. He notched 60 goals and 50 assists, setting new Vancouver records for goals and points. The sale of No. 10 jerseys began to surpass even those of Trevor Linden's. Pavel-mania had gripped the city of Vancouver. Bure matched his own Canucks scoring record the next season, in 1993-94. His most memorable goal in a Canucks uniform, however, was one scored in the playoffs that season. In game seven versus the Calgary Flames, Bure adeptly took a breakaway pass from defenceman Jeff Brown in double overtime and accelerated past a Calgary defender. He deked Calgary netminder Mike Vernon with a move that put an exclamation mark beside one of the most memorable comebacks in NHL history.

Heading into the championship series, the Russian Rocket was leading the post-season with 13 goals. "He's the most talented player I've ever seen," Canucks captain Trevor Linden proclaimed. Although the Canucks lost in the thrilling finals, Bure finished with MVP numbers: 16 goals and 15 assists in 24 games.

During the lockout-shortened 1994-95 season, Bure still managed 20 goals and 23 assists. The next season, 1995-96, a pall of darkness descended over the Canucks. Bure was checked behind the net by Blackhawks defenceman Steve Smith. He tore the anterior cruciate ligament in his right knee, ending his season after just 15 games.

As he stepped onto the ice for the 1996-97 campaign, Bure didn't appear to possess the same game-breaking speed that haunted the dreams of NHL defencemen. He finished the season with 23 goals and 32 assists, playing in just 63 games. He suffered the lingering effects of a whiplash injury sustained in the first game of the season when Calgary Flames defenceman Todd Simpson had checked him headfirst into the boards. But Bure's injury woes wouldn't be the hot topic of conversation among Vancouver hockey fans for long.

In August of 1997, *Province* columnist Gallagher broke

the biggest story in team history. He reported that Bure had met with Pat Quinn to ask for a trade. Bure didn't deny the story. His mysterious life away from the rink included a rumoured marriage of convenience to an American upon his arrival in the U.S. There were also allegations that he had blackmailed the team for a new contract by threatening to sit out during the 1994 playoffs. Kerry Banks, the Vancouver author of *Pavel Bure: The Riddle of The Russian Rocket*, spent a year researching the enigmatic star, hitting roadblocks on the way. "When he heard I was doing a book on Bure, one hockey writer said to me, 'If Bure finds out, he'll probably have somebody break your legs.' He wasn't smiling when he said it. Whether or not his belief has any basis in truth, it does indicate one unsettling aspect of the way Bure is regarded."

Perhaps most intriguing of the rumours are those of Bure's ties with the Russian mafia. In 1996, the U.S. sports television network ESPN broadcast a report alleging that Bure's business partner in his family's watch-making business, Anzor Kikalichvili, was a Russian mob kingpin. Bure acknowledged hearing the allegations about Kikalichvili but denied the validity of the reports. Canucks general manager Pat Quinn responded, "We're fact-finding right now. Everyone here was kind of surprised."

The allegations resurfaced in 1999 during an investigative report by the CBC's *The Fifth Estate*. Bure denied having a position with 21st Century, a business owned by Kikalichvili. The program later showed the company's Moscow billboards that featured Bure and Kikalichvili together. Bure disavowed any association with organized crime, saying, "Trying to clear your name after such false information was like trying to wash yourself from so much dirt."

But Vancouver hockey fans seemed more shocked to learn of Pavel Bure's trade request than they were to learn of any association he might have with the Russian mafia. Apparently, Quinn had told Bure he would be traded after his first request in 1997. The Vancouver general manager was unable to keep his word after being fired.

Playing for coach Mike Keenan, Bure reiterated his request for a trade. Their dealings grew cold. During a road game against the Ottawa Senators on March 20, 1998, Keenan called Bure a "selfish little suck" after a listless first-period effort. When Bure scored a goal and returned to the bench, he was congratulated by the coach. Bure swore at him.

Despite his volatile relationship with Keenan, Bure appeared to fans as his same old game-breaking self. On April 17, he scored his 50th goal of the season against the Calgary Flames in a 4-2 loss. Two nights later, Bure scored the Canucks' lone goal against the Toronto Maple Leafs in a 2-1 loss. It was his final game as a Vancouver Canuck at General Motors Place.

During the summer of 1998, Bure announced publicly that he wanted out of Vancouver. The Russian star didn't deign to say why exactly as he returned to Russia. He said only that he wouldn't fulfil the final year of his contract with the Canucks. The arrival of a man who was part of the management team that originally brought Bure to Vancouver — new GM Brian Burke — didn't diffuse the situation. Bure refused to return to Vancouver, instead working out with his old Red Army team.

"The question everybody wondered about was why he wanted to leave," said his biographer, Banks. "Bure didn't help because he would never articulate. It was pretty obvious it was the dickering over the contract that bugged him and he didn't like Vancouver. He preferred to live in a bigger city that had a Russian community, like New York or Los Angeles. I think it was pretty simple. He also knew the team was getting worse. It's just the Russian way of trying to force the team to do what they want."

Burke, however, refused to be forced into action, saying he would trade Bure when it suited him. That day was January 17, 1999, when Burke sent the Rocket to Florida in a seven-player deal that brought blue-chip defenceman Ed Jovanovski from Florida. Bure's inexplicable trade demand vexed Vancouver Canucks fans. The superstar who had made Pavel a fashionable name for B.C. newborns became a hockey villain.

Bure made his Panther debut on January 21. Sporting borrowed equipment, the travel-weary Bure nevertheless displayed his usual flair, scoring a pair of goals in just 12:09 minutes of ice time. The first goal was vintage Bure, splitting the defense and deking Islander netminder Felix Potvin.

"It was just like Calgary, wasn't it," Bure said to Vancouver reporter Gallagher after the game. He was referring to his first goal, which looked much like his double OT winner in 1994. "I didn't think about it at the time. I just saw space and went for the breakaway." A knee injury limited Bure to just 11 games with Florida. He made the most of each shift, though, scoring 13 goals and adding three assists. During the 1999-00 campaign, Bure played in 74 games, notching 58 goals and 36 points.

Bure's return to General Motors Place came nearly two years after the trade, on October 16, 2001. The 16,859 fans in attendance booed loudly each time Bure touched the puck. Unfazed, Bure scored at 1:36 of the second period. He gave Florida a 1-0 lead after putting a backhander behind Vancouver goaltender Dan Cloutier. Scorned Vancouver fans got the last cheer, however. Cloutier stoned Bure on an overtime breakaway to preserve a 2-2 tie.

Chapter 4
Gino Odjick:
The Algonquin
Assassin

t the 1990 NHL Entry Draft held at B.C. Place Stadium in Vancouver, even Gino Odjick was surprised when the Canucks called his name. It happened in the fifth round and drew a smattering of cheers from the 19,127 in attendance. One round earlier, the Canucks had selected left-winger Darin Bader with their 65th pick of the draft. Odjick, figuring he'd have to sit through several more rounds on an empty stomach before hearing his name, left the stadium to grab a quick bite. "I was having a hot dog when I got drafted," Odjick laughed. "They usually have a break after the fourth round so I went across the street. I was ranked in the ninth round so I thought I had a lot of time. Somebody said, 'Hey you were

just drafted.' Everybody was looking for me."

When Odjick finally made it down to the Canucks' draft table, he extended a big, scarred mitt to shake hands with his NHL employers. All his new coach, Bob McCammon, could say was, "Geez, we had to draft you. Ron Delorme was pouting ever since the second round every time we picked someone else, we finally had to draft you. You better do a good job in camp, kid."

Odjick made his NHL debut with No. 66 stitched on the back of his jersey, but nobody expected him to play like Mario Lemieux. That's not why Canucks amateur scout Ron Delorme persuaded general manager Pat Quinn to select Odjick with the 86th pick. Odjick had racked up 558 penalty minutes in two seasons with the Laval Titans of the Quebec Major Junior Hockey League, earning himself the nickname, "the Algonquin Assassin."

Delorme convinced the Canucks' management to invest in the brave forward that NHL Central Scouting had projected only as a ninth-round prospect. Delorme, himself a veteran of 524 NHL games and a recipient of 667 PIMs, knew what it took to stick in the league as a tough guy. Perhaps he saw a bit of himself in Odjick. Or maybe he saw other qualities in Odjick that other scouts missed. "Odjick had a real strong Memorial Cup and Ronny was really pushing for him," recalled Brian Burke. "He was emphatic that this kid was more than just a tough guy, that he was going to be a player."

Although the scout had no doubt about Odjick, some

in the organization had reservations. Odjick erased them. "During the Memorial Cup, we saw that he had an excellent shot which none of us had appreciated before, other than Ronnie. And he actually played his position fairly well up and down the wing. It was apparent that he was a better player than we thought," Burke said.

At his first training camp with the Vancouver Canucks, the 6-foot-3, 215-pound full-blooded Algonquin Native turned some heads. He was eager to drop the gloves. During a pre-season, all-rookie game in Calgary, Burke realized that the Canucks hadn't squandered their fifth-round draft pick: "He fought Terry Clark, Wendel Clark's brother, he fought Paul Kruse, he fought everybody."

The Canucks still decided to send him to the minors, although he could have played as an overage player for Laval. Burke admitted he was a little apprehensive about giving Odjick the news. "I remember saying to Mike Penny, 'Look if he comes off that chair and starts a fight with me, you've got to jump in here and give me a hand.' Then I told Gino, 'You've had an excellent camp but we're sending you to Milwaukee.' I'm wondering how he's going to take this news and he looks at me and says, 'I don't have to go back to Laval?' I said nope and he pumped his arm in the air like after you score a goal, he was so excited to get a shot at pro hockey."

Dispatched to the Canucks' International Hockey League farm club, the Milwaukee Admirals, the young heavyweight was told to work on his hockey skills and let his injured right hand heal. Odjick took Burke's advice and learned to throw punches as a southpaw. He got into 20 fights in just 17 games with the Admirals. After scoring a career-high 12 goals as a junior in 1989-90, Odjick continued to score on the farm. He netted seven goals and three assists to go along with his 102 penalty minutes. The Canucks kept a close tab on Odjick's progress in the minors. They were without a natural heavyweight in their lineup.

When Pat Quinn arrived to take over the Canucks in 1987, the big Irishman had inherited a last-place team that lacked toughness. Quinn was a former hardrock defenceman who started his coaching career piloting the brawling Philadelphia Flyers. He found the situation as difficult to stomach as a cheap cigar. Although the Canucks had rugged defenceman Garth Butcher, that was all. Quinn bristled as he watched the Canucks' diminutive forwards Dan Quinn, Robert Kron, Steve Bozek, and Brian Bradley get pushed around. After watching the Flames bully the Canucks during a November 19 tilt, Quinn had had enough.

Two days later, Odjick's phone woke him at five a.m. Milwaukee general manager Phil Whittliff told the sleepy winger that the Canucks had recalled him. Driving to the airport, the rookie asked the GM how long he'd be in Vancouver. Whittliff, a former player who'd been with the Admirals organization since 1972, said: "It's up to you. They called Babe Ruth up on an emergency basis for one game and he stayed in the majors his whole career."

If Odjick was going to stay with the team, he knew he'd need some rest. "I just remember thinking, I better sleep on the flight because I won't get a chance to sleep when I get to Vancouver. I slept the whole way." His flight landed in Vancouver just hours prior to the Canucks' face-off against the Chicago Blackhawks. Veteran Canuck Stan Smyl picked him up at the airport. If he was nervous, the Algonquin Assassin didn't show it. "I knew it would be a whole lot easier in the NHL than it was in the minors," Odjick said. He'd been squaring off against some pretty tough customers — mostly using his left hand. "There was Tony Twist, Link Gaetz, Wendel Clark's brother. I think the guys were tougher in the minors than in the NHL at that time."

When they arrived at the Pacific Coliseum, Odjick realized his stay in Vancouver might be short-lived. "I went into the dressing room and looked at my jersey and it was number 66. That was my training camp number," remembered Odjick. High-digit training camp numbers usually meant the player wasn't expected to make the team. "I thought I better not say anything about this, my first game."

Before the seven o'clock face-off, Canucks trainer Pat O'Neill gave him some gloves that matched his new uniform. Odjick took the opportunity to ask if he'd been called up because the team had injuries. "He told me they got pushed around pretty good against Calgary the game before and Pat Quinn got mad and told Ron Delorme, 'We're bringing up your boy.' So I figured they weren't bringing me up for my goal scoring."

Like most Canadian boys, Odjick had dreamed of playing pro hockey. Growing up on the Kitigan Zizi reserve in Maniwaki, Quebec, Odjick always remembered a visit from Montreal Canadiens forward John Chabot. Chabot, from Summerside, P.E.I., was also a Native who'd played in the Quebec Major Junior Hockey League (QMJHL). "It was inspiring to see someone with the same background. I remember Ted Nolan coming too. They achieved their dreams. When you're from an isolated community like we were, it's not until you actually see them or talk to them that you tend to believe it's possible."

If he didn't play professional hockey, Odjick would have probably joined his father, Joe, as a highrise steelworker. "If it's 15 storeys or more, they hire Indians to do the steel work because we're not afraid of heights," he explained. His father toiled for years above Manhattan. "He left Sunday at 7 p.m. to get working Monday at 8 in New York. He left work on Friday at 4 p.m. and got home at 2 or 3 in the morning." When Odjick Sr. came home from work on the weekends, the firewood still had to be done and the hay had to be brought in. "He taught us how to work, that's for sure. If I wouldn't have been a hockey player, I would have done it."

After playing mostly for his reserve hockey team as a youngster, Odjick had been ignored by junior teams at the Bantam Draft. He was preparing to take welding classes at Ottawa's Algonquin College so he could join his father when the phone rang. "One of my school teachers had moved to the city and his son was playing for a tier two team in Ontario. They were short on players so he asked Bob Hartley, who was coaching the Hawkesbury Hawks, to give me a tryout."

Odjick made the cut and suited up for 40 games, scoring two goals and four assists and piling up 167 penalty minutes. Odjick's toughness caught the attention of Pierre Creamer, coach of the QMJHL's Laval Titans. Visits from Chabot and Nolan may have prompted Odjick to dream about a career in pro hockey, but it wasn't until his second season at Laval that he began to believe he could make it as an NHL heavyweight. "People around me told me I had a chance to be an enforcer at the NHL level if I wanted to. I started doing a lot of push-ups and sit-ups."

Like his boyhood idol, Stan Jonathan, Odjick knew he'd have to fight his way into the league. "I knew my role. The first thing a team asks you when you're an enforcer before you're drafted is, are you willing to do the enforcer role at the pro level?" This is because sometimes players play the role in junior and then try to change their game when they get to the pro level. Odjick told the team, "Well, I'd rather be an enforcer than go to work on the highrises with my dad. I'll have no problem doing this role."

As he stepped onto the freshly cleaned sheet of ice at the Pacific Coliseum for the pre-game skate on November 21, Odjick was quickly reminded of why he was there. He felt the hardened stares of a trio of Chicago Blackhawks enforcers sizing him up. "I was really nervous when I went out on the ice and took warm-up, I was shooting pucks around and I could just tell I had Mike Peluso, [Stu] Grimson and [Dave] Manson looking at me thinking 'Who is this kid? Let's fight him tonight and see what he's got.'"

On his first shift in the NHL, Odjick skated in front of the Chicago net and was cross-checked by smashmouth defenceman Dave Manson. Welcome to the NHL. "So right away I got into that first fight. I wasn't really pleased with that one," Odjick recalled. He wanted a more decisive victory. Early in the third period, Odjick nailed Chicago enforcer Stu "The Grim Reaper" Grimson with a good, clean bodycheck. "Then we squared off and got going. I hit him with a couple of good punches and kind of buckled him a few times and as I was walking off the ice, I could hear the 'Gino-Gino' chant." Bob McCammon said to him, "Well kid, I guess you're going to be here for a while."

Odjick was fearless, answering the bell against all the NHL's heavyweight contenders during his first season. He was even prepared to square off against Saddam Hussein.

Ojdick's triumphant heavyweight debut against the Hawks had come during the first Gulf War. An inspired Canucks fan had scrawled a sign that read: "Gino is tougher than Saddam." Seeing the sign during the warm-up, Odjick asked McCammon to point out Saddam Hussein. "I was just coming out of the reserve and we didn't have cable," explained Odjick, smiling. "I was looking around the ice and saying, where the hell is this Saddam Hussein guy?"

Later, when the Canucks played the Los Angeles Kings, Burke needlessly worried about his young pugilist being ready to take on one of the NHL's top enforcers. "He'd fought everyone in the IHL but you don't know if he's ready for a guy like Marty [McSorley]," said Burke. "As soon as they got on the ice, Gino charged the point and fought him. And then we went into Edmonton and he fought Dave Brown three times. This guy was legitimate heavyweight tough."

A cult hockey hero was born. Fans began chanting "Gino-Gino-Gino" from their seats inside the Pacific Coliseum every time Odjick stepped onto the ice. On November 27, Odjick scored his first NHL goal in a 1-1 tie against the Minnesota North Stars. The moment was especially gratifying for Odjick. As he dug the puck out of the net, he acknowledged his parents, who had been flown in for the game by the Canucks organization. "My dad still has the puck. I pointed up to him," he recalled proudly. Odjick, who grew up with five sisters, said his father used to travel everywhere with him. "I remember going to tournaments and we'd pick him up on the side of the road because he'd be coming back from New York to go to the tournaments."

By the end of the 1990-91 season, Odjick had been unofficially inducted into the Canucks' tough-guy hall of fame, alongside other all-time fan favourites like Dave "Tiger" Williams and Ron "The Chief" Delorme. In 45 games, the Algonquin Assassin had scored seven goals. Perhaps more importantly, he had racked up 296 penalty minutes, most of them fighting majors. Odjick won many of the decisions, developing a rep as one of the toughest heavyweights in the league.

Ron Delorme, Odjick's biggest champion at the draft table, had become a mentor for Odjick when he arrived in the NHL. The pair shared a common heritage and NHL job description. Delorme, a Cree from North Battleford, Saskatchewan, had played nine seasons in the NHL and was known more for his fists than his goal-scoring ability. His fierce scrap with Chicago Blackhawks tough guy Grant Mulvey in game five of the 1982 Clarence Campbell final had been a highlight for fans. He constantly shared his tips with his young acolyte. "Ron Delorme showed me this trick with five-pound weights where you punch 100 times as fast as you can. So when you get in a fight, you can punch really fast," recalled Odjick.

Adjusting to the role of NHL enforcer wasn't the only hurdle Odjick faced. He was, after all, from an isolated reserve where he knew his neighbours. His pastimes included hunting for moose or riding snowmobiles. "Living in a very tight-knit reservation, we had our own way of life and own way of thinking and we're very traditional to our Algonquin culture," Odjick said. In the big city of Vancouver, by contrast, he said, "You don't know where you're going. You don't know where you are."

Once he was in the NHL, though, Pat Quinn taught him

"how to be a professional and how to be the best human being possible." Brian Burke also helped. Odjick arrived in Vancouver sporting his best sweater and slacks. He didn't own a suit or tie. "When we went on the road to play our pre-season games, he had no clothes," Burke recalled. "Someone went out and bought him a sports coat and he wore that sports coat every day on the road."

After Odjick was called up from the farm, Burke gave Stan Smyl a couple thousand dollars to take Odjick shopping. "You can't come to NHL games without suits and ties and I didn't have any," Odjick recalled. "He knew if he only bought me one, I'd be wearing the same suit every day." Burke's help extended beyond expanding Odjick's wardrobe. "He really took care of his players. He was like a dad, nobody touched his players."

Odjick recalled one particular night at the Calgary Saddledome after he'd broken his right hand during a fight with a Calgary Flames rookie. In the concourse area of the rink, he was met by Flames general manager Doug Risebrough. The former NHL agitator challenged him to a fight. Brian Burke arrived from the press box shortly after-wards. "Burke told him, 'If you're going to go with anybody, you're going to go with me.' Doug changed his mind and went back up the stairs."

During his second season in Vancouver, Odjick became more comfortable with his West Coast surroundings. He moved to the Musqueam Reserve near the University of

British Columbia. He struck up a friendship with new teammate Pavel Bure, who was also finding it difficult to fit in. Nobody could have predicted a more unlikely friendship. The players were as different on the ice as they were off it. But they were disparate souls drawn together by a shared feeling of culture shock and alienation. "He came over from Russia and he was a Red Russian, very proud of his heritage, and when he came I knew the feeling he had. I started teaching him how to speak English. We were two people who came from completely different cultures than what we were put into."

The friendship blossomed on the ice, too. Both players excelled at the roles they were being paid for. It wasn't long, though, before they learned from each other through osmosis. Odjick scored a career-high 16 goals and 29 points, including five game-winners. Many of them were assisted by Bure during the 1993-94 season. Bure learned how to protect himself when Odjick wasn't in the lineup. During game two of the second-round playoff match-up against the Dallas Stars in 1994, Bure retaliated against the constant abuse he was getting from the Stars. He viciously elbowed tough guy Shane Churla to the ice in the first period. Afterward, Bure was fined $500 by the NHL for his hit. "It's not my style, but I had no choice. They're trying to kill me. I'm lucky I didn't get hurt."

Odjick dressed in only 10 games during the 1994 Stanley Cup playoff run. In those days, the enforcers didn't play in too many playoff games. His most memorable moments in a Canucks uniform often preceded a trip to the sin bin. The Maniwaki Mauler recorded more than 100 penalty minutes in each of his eight seasons with the Canucks. He rewrote the team record book as the most penalized player in club history. His 2127 minutes — the equivalent of more than 35 games — eclipsed Garth Butcher's previous record of 1668 minutes. Odjick also holds the Canucks' record for single-game and single-period penalty minutes. He amassed 47 minutes during an on-ice meltdown against the Los Angeles Kings on November 12, 1992.

Odjick racked up the majority of his career penalty minutes against regular Smythe Division foes like Edmonton Oilers tough guy Dave Brown and Los Angeles Kings police-man Marty McSorley. Interestingly, it was New York Ranger and Toronto Maple Leaf enforcer Tie Domi whom Odjick least liked to take on. "I didn't like fighting Tie Domi because you had to punch down and he had such good balance. Plus you couldn't hurt him. He's probably one of the guys as enforcer you have the most respect for. He's only five-foot-nine and he's taken all comers his entire career. Believe me he's taken a lot of punches. He's turned out to be a pretty good player."

Odjick turned out to be a pretty good player, too, just as his mentor Delorme had predicted. Towards the end of his career, he was playing 10 to 12 minutes per game and scoring 8 to 10 times a year. "That was the goal. I never wanted to fight just to see if I was tougher than one guy. I never wanted to be known as the toughest guy in the NHL. I just wanted to be known as a guy that took care of his teammates."

During his tenure in Vancouver, Odjick won the respect of his teammates, coaches, and the fans. But after the firing of Pat Quinn, Odjick found himself in a scrap that he couldn't possibly win. "I was devastated," Odjick recalled, hearing the news. "Me and Pavel were both so mad and disappointed and we knew we wouldn't be around for much longer. We didn't want to be part of it. Although there were times that Pavel and Pat butted heads, Pavel always knew Pat brought the best out of him. He played his best hockey for Pat Quinn, same with myself."

Mike Keenan's arrival in Vancouver was a harbinger of change for the Canucks. The Algonquin Assassin made the mistake of defending his old pal, Trevor Linden, against Keenan's verbal abuse. While others stared at their skates, Odjick just did what he'd been programmed to do his entire career — stand up for his teammates. "There is no use in slandering Trevor Linden or embarrassing a guy who has devoted his heart and soul to this team," Gino Odjick said later. "I know for a fact that Trevor goes all out every time he laces on the skates. In the eight years I've been here, there's no player I respect more than Trevor Linden."

Odjick's staunch public support of Linden succeeded in showing up Keenan in much the same way the coach had ridiculed the former captain. Keenan wasn't amused. On March 23, 1998, Odjick was traded to the New York Islanders in exchange for defenceman Jason Strudwick. Predictably,

Pavel Bure was upset. "He's my best friend and I'm really disappointed," Bure told Vancouver reporters. "Some people say he's not a great hockey player, but he's one of the toughest players in the NHL and he got 15 goals when he played with me. He's part of Canucks history."

One day later, Odjick came out at General Motors Place wearing an unfamiliar Islanders jersey. In the first period, he dropped the gloves with Strudwick, the player who replaced him in the Vancouver lineup. He won the fight easily. A familiar chant erupted from the stands, "Gino-Gino."

Chapter 5
Captains Canuck: Linden and Smyl

uring a pre-game ceremony on November 3, 1991, Stan Smyl's No. 12 jersey slowly inched toward the rafters of the Pacific Coliseum. Newly appointed Canucks captain Trevor Linden slapped his Bauer hockey stick against the boards. He joined the sell-out standing crowd to pay homage to "the Steamer" one last time.

For the long-suffering Canucks fans, it was an emotional moment. Smyl, the longest-serving captain in team history, had played his entire 13-year NHL career with the Canucks. He retired as the team's all-time leader in games played (896), goals (262), assists (411), and points (673). Unofficially, Smyl was also the team's all-time leader in hits, heart, and hustle. During an era of on-ice mediocrity, his hard-nosed play had given Vancouver fans at least one thing to cheer about every time he was on the ice. "He was really all there was, oftentimes he was the only reason to go and see a game," recalled *Province* sportswriter Tony Gallagher. "He played so hard every night. He took so many of the losses to heart, as though it was his fault as captain."

Standing at centre ice with his wife Jennifer and his three children, Smyl was also choking back tears. He told the fans, "You made me a better player and a better person. The faith that you had in the Steamer made the game worthwhile to me."

Smyl had been selected 40th overall by the Canucks at the 1978 NHL Amateur Draft. Not even Canucks general manager Jake Milford could have predicted that Smyl's jersey would one day be retired by the team. In fact, when Smyl arrived at training camp, few believed that the five-foot-eight winger with the awkward skating style had a shot at making the team, let alone become the team's captain and leading scorer.

The NHL scouts who doubted him probably hadn't seen Smyl play night after night for the New Westminster Bruins. The feisty winger developed a redoubtable reputation as a fierce bodychecker with a booming slap shot. He'd led the Bruins to three Memorial Cup appearances. In 1978, after his team won its second straight junior championship, he took home the Stafford Smythe Memorial Trophy as the tournament's MVP. Fixated on measuring height and weight, goals and assists, the scouts had overlooked the fact that there wasn't a caliper device for measuring a player's heart.

Smyl left his home in Glendon, Alberta, as a young teenager to play for the B.C. Junior Hockey League's Bellingham Blazers, a feeder team to the Western Canada Hockey League's New West Bruins. By the time he was 15, Stan had told his mom, "I don't want to go to school. I want to be a hockey player." Legendary Bruins coach Ernie "Punch" McLean recognized Smyl's potential the moment he pulled a Blazers jersey over his head. "I said he would make it to the National Hockey League, not on his skill level at that time, but on his heart."

At his first NHL training camp, Smyl ran over Harold Snepsts. He dropped the Canucks' big blueliner with a thud, grabbing the attention of his teammates and first-year head coach Harry Neale. "Here was this rookie coming in and starting to bang people in training camp, this really got everybody's attention and pissed off a few people. But he didn't back down and he kept running around and he did it from the first day he was there and played himself onto the team," recalled Gallagher. "He was a third-round pick, I don't think he was expected to make the team. We knew who he was and what he brought to the table but no one expected him to make the team. Nobody knew the offensive skills he had with the big shot."

Chris Oddleifson, who captained the Canucks in 1976-77, was among the veterans who took notice. Smyl's jarring hit on the team's undisputed physical leader was "the precursor of his career," he said. "He was going to play the game hard."

At the beginning of the 1978-79 season, the Vancouver Canucks stepped onto the ice sporting garish new uniforms. Behind the bench stood an unknown coach named Harry Neale. A new all-rookie line featured Smyl, Swedish import Thomas Gradin, and left-winger Curt Fraser. The new line received better opening-night reviews than the untraditional yellow "V" uniforms. They combined for six points in an 8-2 shellacking of the Colorado Rockies.

Thirteen years later, as Smyl was being feted at centre ice with a brand new van, a Harley Davidson, and a portrait by North Vancouver artist Glen Green, despairing fans rewound the highlight reel of the Steamer's career. During the 1979-80 season, Smyl had led Vancouver with 31 goals, 47 assists, 78 points, and 204 penalty minutes — the last time any NHLer topped his club in these four categories. Smyl's career included three 30-plus goal seasons. In a memorable trip to the Stanley Cup championship in 1982, he scored nine goals and nine assists in 17 games.

Smyl scored just 10 goals in his final three seasons with the Canucks. But he knew the crash course in leadership that he had given to a callow rookie named Trevor Linden was more important for the organization. "From the first day I met him, I could always tell there was something special about Trevor as a player, but even more so as a person," Smyl said.

Stan Smyl

Outwardly, the two had little in common. Stan Smyl was short and stocky. Trevor Linden was tall and lean. Smyl served his junior apprenticeship over 900 kilometres from his Alberta birthplace, Linden played for his hometown junior squad. Linden had the boy-next-door good looks; Smyl's nose looked like a door had hit it. Smyl was a steam engine fuelled by coal, Linden a V-12 running on premium gasoline. One was picked 40th and hoped to make the team; the other was picked second overall and expected to make the team better.

Linden was a prototype power forward with a 6-foot-4, 220-pound frame. He was the building-block player that Canucks general manager Pat Quinn dreamed about selecting with the second-overall pick at the 1988 NHL Entry Draft. NHL Central Scouting had ranked Mike Modano, a high-scoring centreman from the Prince Albert Raiders, the top pick at the draft. But, according to Brian Burke, "With Pat being in charge, we probably would have taken Trevor anyway. We all respected Mike Modano as a player and saw the offensive gifts that Trevor didn't have. We knew Trevor would be a solid two-way player."

Prior to the draft, the Canucks had brought in all of the top picks, subjecting them to a battery of physical and psychological tests. Modano's interviews with the team were almost flawless. "A great kid," Burke recalled, noting that an assistant coach had doubts only about Modano's choirboy mug. "Jack McIlhargey interviewed him and said, 'We can't take him. He doesn't have one scar on his face.'"

Linden's pre-draft interview didn't go as well. Burke remembered him calling the night before to say, "'My dad said I have to call you because I can't come in for the testing tomorrow.' So right away I thought OK, Lou Nanne [GM of the North Stars] is screwing around here. He's going to take him because Minnesota had the first pick." But the young prospect went on to explain that he had to help with the young bulls on his uncle's ranch. Burke asked him, "What's your job? He says, 'Well, I grab these young bulls by the neck, wrestle them to the ground, and hold them while they brand them and cut their nuts off.'" What could Burke say but, "That's no problem Trevor."

Linden's team-first mentality wasn't the only character trait the Canucks coveted.

When the Canucks drafted Linden, his junior coach at Medicine Hat, Barry Melrose, figured that the Canucks had acquired a future leader. "I expect him to become the captain in Vancouver in about three years," Melrose said at the time. "He's had that [leadership quality] his whole life. He's a character kid. I think you'll see Vancouver got the best player in the draft."

Melrose's bold prediction made sense. As a swizzle-stick-thin teenager with the Medicine Hat Tigers in the Western Hockey League, Linden had carried the team to back-to-back Memorial Cups. In his final season in Medicine Hat, Linden showed scouts that he could also score, netting 46 goals and 64 assists in 67 games. And, as Vancouver Canucks fans would soon find out, Linden's favourite season was the spring. In 16 playoff games with the Tigers that season, Linden scored 13 goals and 12 assists.

A teammate of Linden's in Medicine Hat, Dallas Stars forward Rob DiMaio, also recognized the leadership potential of his teammate early on. "Even when he was 16, 17, when I was with him, he carried himself so much older. He was a mature kid. That's why he was a captain at such a young age and he's continued to be a leader throughout his career. He's first class. Guys look up to him."

During Linden's first training camp with the Canucks in Parksville, B.C., the battle-tested veteran Smyl took him under his wing. Linden acknowledged the influence of Smyl's professionalism on and off the ice. Smyl was a good example for him, Gallagher agreed. He would look out onto the ice and see how hard Smyl played. In terms of skill, however, Gallagher said, "Trevor was thought to have a lot more than Stan and a lot more potential."

Trevor had greater expectations placed on him, too. The team had been so unsuccessful that they had received the second overall pick the preceding year. That showed what kind of shape they were in. They were looking for a lift, and Linden provided it. The 18-year-old finished the 1988-89 season tied for the team lead in goals (30) and second in points (59). He became the first rookie in club history to score 30 goals and be named the team's MVP. The *Hockey News* selected Linden as their rookie of the year. He finished second behind New York Rangers Brian Leetch for the NHL's Calder Trophy, awarded to the league's top rookie.

And like Bobby Clarke, the former gap-toothed Flyers

captain with whom he was compared, Linden played hard when it mattered the most — the Stanley Cup playoffs. In his rookie season, Linden appeared in all seven games of the first-round matchup against the heavily favoured Calgary Flames. Although Calgary won the dramatic series on a controversial overtime goal (scored by crease-crashing centre Joel Otto, just after Smyl's breakaway had been stopped by Calgary goaltender Mike Vernon), Linden proved his playoff mettle. The gangly rookie counted three goals and four assists against the eventual 1989 Stanley Cup champions.

Despite struggling through a minor "sophomore jinx" in 1989-90, Linden finished fifth in team scoring with 51 points and 21 goals. The next season, he became the youngest player to make an appearance at the mid-season NHL all-star game and he led the Canucks team in points.

Before the start of the 1991-92 season, Pat Quinn decided it was time for Stan Smyl's heir-apparent to be named officially. After alternating with teammates Doug Lidster and Dan Quinn the year before, Trevor Linden became the full-time captain of the Canucks. In just his fourth season in the NHL, at 21 years of age, Linden was the youngest captain in the league at the time. The Medicine Hat native thrived under the new pressure and the 'C' over his heart. For the second consecutive year, he led the team in scoring, this time with 75 points. His 31 goals ranked him second on the team.

With Linden's leadership and the arrival of Soviet superstar Pavel Bure in Vancouver in 1991-92, Pat Quinn had assembled the underpinnings of a playoff contender in Vancouver. The Canucks closed out the regular season with a 4-4 draw against arch-rival Calgary on April 16. Setting franchise records with 42 wins and 96 points, the team finished first overall in the Smythe.

After defeating the Winnipeg Jets 4-3 in the first round, the Canucks faced the Mark Messier-led Edmonton Oilers. They lost this series 4-2. The next season, the Canucks' Stanley Cup playoff education continued with a second-round loss to the Los Angeles Kings. Eventually, the Canucks would put the playoff lessons to good use, with Trevor Linden standing at the front of the class.

Linden's definitive moment as captain Canuck came during a miraculous springtime of 1994. Exactly 12 years earlier, Stan Smyl had led the Canucks to an improbable trip to New York in the Stanley Cup final against the Islanders. During the 1994 playoffs, Linden was finally able to grow a playoff beard. He also displayed an enviable combination of leadership, grit, and clutch goal-scoring. If Stan Smyl had been "Captain Crunch," Trevor Linden was "Captain Clutch." Linden finished the 1994 Stanley Cup playoffs with 12 goals and 13 assists in 24 playoff games. His overtime winner against Calgary goalie Mike Vernon forced a seventh and deciding game against the Flames. Against the high-powered New York Rangers, Linden's game seven performance was perhaps the grittiest and most determined of the team's 34-year history. With the Canucks trailing 2-0 after the first

Trevor Linden

period, Linden scored a short-handed goal at 5:21. Mark Messier scored on the power play to make it 3-1. Then Linden scored again on a tremendous individual effort, with 15:10 remaining in the third, to make the score 3-2.

"Trevor is one of those players who rises to all occasions," said defenceman Dave Babych. "Those playoffs were one of them. In game seven, he had guys crawling all over his back and he's still scoring goals. When you can still perform like that, it says a lot for the person. There's a lot of guys who do a lot of talking but a large percentage of them don't follow up in the ice, and he certainly did that, he's done it tenfold over the years."

Although he lost out that time, Linden probably figured he'd get another chance to have his name engraved on Lord Stanley's Cup. Especially after the Canucks signed coveted free agent Mark Messier on July 28, 1997. Messier, after all, had willed the Rangers to the 1994 NHL championship, breaking New York's 54-year Stanley Cup drought. Could he do it for the Canucks?

In 1997, the Canucks travelled to Tokyo, Japan, to face the Anaheim Mighty Ducks in the first-ever NHL game to be played outside North America. Linden chose this "Game One '97" to pass over the team captaincy to Messier with his fistful of Stanley Cup rings. Linden's team-first gesture would later be rewarded with a check-from-behind. Less than a month later, on November 4, 1997, Orca Bay officials fired the man who had drafted Linden and made him the team's ninth team captain.

Predictably, Linden took the news about Quinn as hard as anyone on the team. "In a sense, I kind of grew up with Pat Quinn," Linden said. "I was just 18 when I came here. I was a boy. I've always looked up to him, definitely. From the day I got here, he was someone I respected and valued his trust."

Almost immediately, new coach Mike Keenan clashed with Trevor Linden. Just two games into the Keenan era, Linden injured his groin in practice and missed the next eight games. He returned to the lineup for a December 8 game against Keenan's former team, the St. Louis Blues. Linden made a point of congratulating the third and fourth liners for their efforts. But Keenan, upset about his team's performance, purportedly berated Linden in an expletive-peppered tirade between periods. A month later, Keenan benched Linden for the third period of a 4-2 loss to Montreal. He later questioned Linden's effort to the media: "Trevor has the ability to be a front-line player and he certainly has to demonstrate to his teammates that he's a lot more committed that he is. Trevor can step up his game unless he's not the hockey player everybody in the country, including Team Canada, thinks he is. He's probably playing at a 50 percent level."

Keenan appeared intent on purging the club of players who made up the nucleus of the 1994 Stanley Cup final team, players he referred to as "Quinn's boys." When his responsibilities were expanded to include the authority to make trades, he started to disband the team. In January 1998, Kirk McLean and Martin Gelinas — two of Linden's closest friends on the team — were sent to Carolina in exchange for Sean Burke, Geoff Sanderson, and Enrico Ciccone. In February, Linden learned from equipment manager Pat O'Neill that Keenan had traded him to the New York Islanders in exchange for Todd Bertuzzi, Bryan McCabe, and a third-round draft pick.

Rather than firing verbal shots at Keenan, Linden handled the difficult situation with the same character and class that had made him such a fan favourite throughout his career. "I have to say things weren't going really well here, the team was struggling and I was as well," Linden told reporters. "I was given a lot of opportunity here and things weren't happening for me. So I think it became a situation that was going to happen and it wasn't the biggest surprise."

Keenan appeared more diplomatic at the news conference announcing the Linden trade than he had been behind closed doors. "We are certainly very appreciative of the efforts he has made in this community and we wish him particularly well in the next two weeks representing Canada at the Olympics," said Keenan. "We also wish him a great career in New York. I told him change is difficult but that the change would be good for him. He's still a young man and he has a bright future ahead of him."

Local fans and sportswriters alike lamented the trade. "This was the ultimate team guy, a player who had switched from right wing to centre and turned over his captaincy for the good of the club, being blamed for all of Vancouver Canucks problems by a coach who had a two-month history with the organization," seethed *Province* columnist Kent Gilchrist. "Besides being one of the best players to ever pull a Canucks jersey over his head, Linden did the community work because he wanted to, not out of a sense of duty to those paying his salary."

Linden's contributions in Vancouver extended beyond the rink. Away from the cameras, Linden regularly visited the B.C. Children's Hospital. He also created the Trevor Linden Foundation. He made contributions to the development of Canuck Place, a hospice for terminally ill kids, and created the Captain's Corner suite to host underprivileged kids at GM Place during home games.

Linden's trade began a mini NHL tour of duty for him. A month after being traded to the Islanders, Linden was named the team captain. Two seasons later, he was dealt to the Montreal Canadiens for a first-round pick in the 1999 draft. In Montreal, he was a leader both on and off the ice for two seasons before being moved to the Washington Capitals in a 2001 deadline deal.

On November 10, 2001, new Vancouver general manger Brian Burke re-acquired the former captain. Burke had been the Canucks' director of hockey operations when Linden was drafted in 1988. "We're very pleased to have Trevor back in Vancouver," Burke enthused. "Our expectation is that Trevor will add versatility, leadership, and experience to our forwards."

Burke wasn't concerned about bringing the former Canucks captain back in a new role: "I talked to him before he got on the plane, after we made the trade and said, 'You know we have a captain [Markus Naslund]. I'm not bringing you back as a captain, I'm bringing you back as a player and a teammate.' He said 'I understand that.' I think Trevor is one of those guys that could make any team situation work. I think he has no ego when it comes to winning hockey games."

Who says you can't come home again? "Any time you are traded, there is some anxiety," Linden said, almost a year after the trade back to Vancouver. "Certainly coming back here was a special situation for obvious reasons. I was a little anxious about …being able to find a home here and fit in and all those things because it was a completely different team from the one I left."

Linden notched his first goal as a renewed Canuck on November 23 at Boston. He finished the season with 12 goals and 22 assists in 64 games. He'd played his best hockey in years and was still the same leader in the dressing room. "He's one of the big leaders on this team," confirmed coach Marc Crawford, a former teammate of Stan Smyl. "He's a very big part of our identity, both past and present, and that can't be understated."

Linden would later say that the trade back to Vancouver had rejuvenated his career. "Last year was the most fun I had playing hockey in four or five years. It was a pretty neat experience." On November 25, 2002, in his first full season back with the Canucks, Linden scored his 263rd goal as a Canuck against Minnesota. He had surpassed his one-time mentor, Stan Smyl, for the team's all-time lead in goals. Linden finished the season with 19 goals — his highest output since his

1995-96 season with the Canucks. Perhaps more importantly, he helped the Canucks reach the second round of the play-offs for the first time since 1995-96.

On March 8, 2004, during the infamous game against the Colorado Avalanche in which Todd Bertuzzi sucker-punched Steve Moore, it was Stan Smyl's turn to applaud his former protégé. Linden's pair of assists in the second period against the Avs gave him 674 regular-season career points. As synonymous with the franchise as No. 12, Linden had finally surpassed his mentor as the top point-getter in Canucks history. Although he wasn't on the ice, Smyl deserved an assist on the play.

Chapter 6
The 1994 Stanley Cup Run

ven a decade later, when asked about the seminal moment of the Canucks' trip to the 1994 Stanley Cup championship series, Vancouver fans offer an almost unanimous response: "The Save."

The Save is Vancouver sporting vernacular shorthand for the overtime stop Kirk McLean made in game seven against the Calgary Flames. It's one of the most memorable, most replayed highlights in the team's 34-year history: McLean flying across the crease, his pads stacked, to save a one-timer off the stick of Flames winger Robert Reichel and preserve a 3-3 tie in overtime. The trigger-happy goal judge had already pressed the red-light button, but McLean's skate toe kicked the puck out at the last second. A video review of the save confirmed the puck had not crossed the line.

The sellout crowd inside the Olympic Saddledome — along with a coast-to-coast *Hockey Night in Canada* audience — watched in disbelief. Breaking down the right wing, Theo Fleury had led the three-on-one rush over the Canucks blueline. As he cruised past the face-off dot, he made a deft cross-ice pass to Reichel, a 40-goal scorer. McLean anticipated the pass. "It's tough not to play the man with the puck [Fleury] and I was able to read him a little, then lay over to the man [Reichel] with the puck," McLean said after the game. "Did I know the red light came on behind me? No. I didn't."

The Save would "rank as one of the all-time saves in playoff history," declared one Calgary reporter. But McLean's game-saving heroics set up another event that Canucks fans consider the other seminal moment in the 1994 Stanley Cup playoffs: The Goal. At 2:20 of the second overtime period in the same game, Pavel Bure received a pinpoint pass from defenceman Jeff Brown that sent him blurring past Flames defenceman Zarley Zalapski. Breaking in alone on Mike Vernon, Bure deked the Flames' netminder and slid the puck in the net. The Canucks' memorable come-from-behind series victory was thus concluded in dramatic fashion. "Most people would pick that as the most dramatic goal that the Canucks have ever had," said the team's legendary play-by-play man Jim Robson.

But before The Save, before The Goal, there was The Curve.

Rewind to game five. After the Canucks had shocked the Flames 5-0 in game one, Calgary easily won the next three contests. Game five at the Olympic Saddledome, most agreed, would likely be the last 60 minutes of hockey for the Vancouver Canucks that spring. "There hardly was a soul who didn't think the series was over, and that would probably include the players," said Robson. At the end of regulation time, the game was tied 1-1, with Pavel Bure recording his first goal of the series. That's when the pivotal moment of the Canucks' Stanley Cup playoffs took place. It didn't happen on the ice, but rather outside the Canucks dressing room, between the third period and the start of overtime.

Canucks left-winger Geoff Courtnall, a 26 goal-scorer during the regular season, stood in a small corridor outside the dressing room working on the blade of his Easton. He used a propane blowtorch to give it a wicked bend. "I stepped on it and put a big curve on it. Pavel was out there with me and he said, 'What are you doin'?' and I said 'If I get one shot, it's going high,'" Courtnall recalled. "The places to shoot on Vernon were high glove and five hole. I just thought that if I got a chance, I'd shoot high."

Courtnall got an opportunity eight minutes into overtime. As he cruised down the boards the puck bounced between Calgary defenceman Kevin Dahl's legs and onto his Easton. Courtnall accelerated towards the Flames goal and wired a slapshot from the face-off circle, past Vernon's outstretched glove hand. "Somebody was cutting me off, so I just

Geoff Courtnall

shot it, over his shoulder," Courtnall recalled.

The dramatic overtime winner was a carbon copy of the goal scored by his former Oilers teammate Wayne Gretzky on Vernon during the 1988 Stanley Cup playoffs. "Wayne scored over Vernon's shoulder. On the same exact shot. On the same play down the wing. I just thought: 'If I get a chance today down the wing, I was going to try him over his shoulder because he comes way out,'" Courtnall told Eric Duhatschek of the *Calgary Herald* after the game. "It's just exciting to go home with life. We were up against the wall."

Jim Robson agreed that Courtnall's goal changed the Canucks' playoff trajectory that year. "His goal made it an overtime win and now the series is three games to two ... it's another series. The Courtnall goal really seemed to bring the team together and gave them new life. That got them going."

The goal extended the series, and the confidence, of the Canucks. "When we started the playoffs, I didn't think we had a chance against Calgary. They were the team favoured to win. We struggled all year for consistency. We had great players but we never seemed to find our stride. In the playoffs, Pat [Quinn] tried some different line combinations to balance things out and it seemed to work," Courtnall recalled.

For Courtnall, the OT winner offered a redemption. Prior to game five, the winger's penchant for the marathon shifts had been singled out during an impassioned speech by the Canucks' coach. "Pat Quinn thought Geoff Courtnall was staying on the ice too long and at the end he'd take a penalty and then take another long shift," recalled teammate Gino Odjick, who played 10 games in the 1994 playoffs. "Pat said in the old days if a soldier disobeyed the general, it would be considered mutiny and they'd put his head on the log, 'I'd cut your head off if we were in those days.' He punched a Gatorade cooler and it went flying. Nobody moved or said a word. And boy, that changed the whole team around. We won the next three games and there was nobody staying out there for long shifts," Odjick laughed. "In my view that's what changed the whole thing around right there. Pat Quinn let us know there was no room for individuals."

And when the big Irishman spoke, players listened. He was an intimidating presence, but he'd also won the respect of his players for his loyalty and the manner in which he treated them. Each player in the dressing room had been brought to the Canucks' organization by Quinn. Many had been offered a second chance in Vancouver, like talented defenceman Jyrki Lumme, whose career had stalled in Montreal. "He liked to teach. He didn't play any head games. When he was pissed off, he would put his fist down. He had respect for the guys. He was the best man for the job by far," said Lumme.

Quinn also had history with Vancouver. He had played for the 1970 expansion Canucks for two seasons before being selected by the Atlanta Flames in the Expansion Draft and later becoming their team captain. He then stepped behind the bench as the coach of the Philadelphia Flyers in 1978-79. He earned the Jack Adams award as the top coach in the NHL one season later, after his team finished with 116 points. After four successful seasons on Broad Street, Quinn left hockey to attend law school. He returned to the NHL as the coach of the Los Angeles Kings in 1984-85. The Griffiths family hired Quinn as GM and VP in 1987. Canuck faithful had, by then, sat through 11 consecutive losing seasons. Before the arrival of Quinn, they'd had little to cheer about except for a surprise trip to the Stanley Cup final in 1982.

The Canucks finally had a hockey czar, but the hiring was mired in controversy. Because Quinn had signed with the Canucks while still under contract with the Kings, the NHL fined the organization $310,000 and suspended Quinn. A British Columbia Supreme Court ruling later reduced the fine to $10,000 and allowed Quinn to assume his role as the team's new president.

The big Irishman set out to rebuild the franchise and change the hockey culture in the Vancouver dressing room. Quinn immediately began adding depth to the talent-thin franchise by swapping one talented player for two or more prospects. He made his most important swap on September 15, 1987, when he traded the team's most talented offensive player, Swede Patrik Sundstrom, to the New Jersey Devils in exchange for Greg Adams and Kirk McLean. Quinn's next underpinning was a lanky winger from the Medicine Hat Tigers named Trevor Linden.

In 1989, under the Quinn regime, the Vancouver Canucks qualified for the Stanley Cup finals for the first time in three seasons. In the opening-round against the first-place Calgary Flames, the Canucks surprised hockey pundits by stretching the series to game seven, losing in a heartbreaking OT.

95

Quinn's knack for acquiring castoffs from other NHL clubs and turning them into valuable contributors became evident in the playoffs that season. Earlier in the year, he had acquired a talented but fragile defenceman, Paul Reinhart, and a useful but undersized forward, Steve Bozek, from Calgary for a third-round draft pick. Both players played prominent roles in the playoffs against Calgary, with Reinhart registering five points in seven games.

Quinn continued to cobble together a Stanley Cup contender at the 1989 NHL Entry Draft in Bloomington, Minnesota. He gambled a sixth-round draft pick on a young Soviet named Pavel Bure. Quinn's "five-year plan" for rebuilding the Canucks franchise began to manifest itself on the ice. During the 1991-92 season, the Canucks finished first in the Smythe Division, setting a franchise record with 96 points. The Canucks continued to improve on the ice in 1992-93, finishing with 101 points, again atop the Smythe. Quinn kept on giving up his proven players in return for packages of lesser stars. No trade was more important than the deadline deal on March 5, 1991. It packaged longtime Canucks blueliner Garth Butcher and forward Dan Quinn in exchange for Cliff Ronning, Sergio Momesso, Geoff Courtnall, and Robert Dirk from St. Louis. Ronning gave the team a deft, play-making centre. Momesso was a robust winger. Courtnall had a knack for scoring key goals, and Dirk was a crease-clearing, stay-at-home defenceman. On that same day, Quinn also acquired defenceman Dana Murzyn from the

Calgary Flames. Expendable in Calgary, Murzyn patrolled the Canucks blueline for years.

Despite the continual upgrade of talent and size, the Canucks had yet to grow a full playoff beard. In 1992, the team rallied from a 3-1 series deficit to defeat the Winnipeg Jets in the Smythe Division semi-final. In the division final, the playoff-tested Edmonton Oilers defeated the Canucks 4-2. A year later, the Canucks again defeated the Jets in the opening round but lost to the Los Angeles Kings in the second round 4-2.

Heading into the 1993-94 season, expectations were rising for the first time among Canuck faithful. Incredibly, Quinn had turned the sad-sack team into a playoff contender. The Canucks started the campaign as the hottest team in the NHL, compiling a 7-1 record. But as the season went sideways, the hoped-for Stanley Cup parade route down Robson Street was cancelled. The team stumbled, finishing the season only one game above .500, and second in the Smythe division. During the season, Quinn was widely criticized for not re-signing Petr Nedved, the Canucks' first pick at the 1991 draft. As the contract stalemate continued, the highly skilled Czech signed with the Blues. On March 14, the Canucks received their compensation: centreman Craig Janney and a second-round pick. Most agreed Quinn had swung a good deal until Janney balked at playing for Vancouver. Quinn was then forced to make a trade for defencemen Jeff Brown and Bret Hedican and rookie forward Nathan La Fayette. The fans decried the trade at the time, but Pat Quinn would later be feted as a hockey genius. His patience and faith in players he had brought to Vancouver was starting to pay off.

After Geoff Courtnall's OT winner against the Flames in game five, it was young captain Trevor Linden's turn to be the hero in game six. Linden moved to centre ice for the Calgary series to help mitigate the Flames' size down the middle. He scored a power-play goal at 16:43 of the first overtime period. The Canucks' 3-2 victory set up Pavel Bure's heroic breakaway deke in game seven. The Canucks had won three straight overtime games.

The Canucks wouldn't have long to savour the victory. Next stop, Dallas. The Stars had finished the regular season seventh overall, seven spots ahead of Vancouver. But Pat Quinn had the team believing. In game one, Martin Gelinas scored the game-winning goal at 15:21 of the third. Kirk McLean stopped 35 pucks as the Canucks won 6-4. McLean posted his second shutout of the playoffs in game two as the Canucks returned to Vancouver leading 2-0. Dallas won game three of the series, 4-3, in Vancouver. The Canucks' overtime streak continued in game four. Sergio Momesso scored at 11:01 of overtime, giving the Canucks an opportunity to advance to the conference semifinals for only the second time in the club's history. Pavel Bure scored twice in game five as the Canucks cruised to a 4-2 victory. After the game, defence-man Jeff Brown said, "When Pavel Bure scored that overtime goal to beat Calgary last series, we pulled together, looked at each other, and realized we had a rare opportunity."

The Canucks faced the Toronto Maple Leafs in the conference final, again opening the series on the road. In game
one, the Canucks found themselves in an unusual position,
losers of an OT game. The Canucks rebounded in game two
with a 4-3 victory. Defenceman Jyrki Lumme scored the
game-winner at 4:14 of the third period, breaking the Leafs'
home ice advantage. Back at the Pacific Coliseum, games
three and four belonged to Kirk McLean. The table-hockey-
style goaltender stopped each of the 29 shots the Leafs fired at
him in both games. The back-to-back shutouts gave McLean
four for the playoffs, equaling an NHL record.

Desperate not to go golfing, the Leafs played a strong
game five. They staked themselves to a 3-0 lead after the
first period on goals by Wendel Clark, Doug Gilmour, and
Mike Eastwood. The Canucks responded with three goals
in the second period. Pavel Bure extended his playoff-scor-
ing streak to a Canuck-record 15 games on a goal by Greg
Adams. Murray Craven and Nathan La Fayette also scored for
the Canucks. Overtime took just 14 seconds to determine the
winner. B.C. native Greg Adams scored on Felix Potvin to earn
the Canucks their first trip to the Stanley Cup since 1982.

"This is unbelievable, this is what you work for, this
is what you dream about," an ecstatic Quinn told reporters
after the game.

Just as it had been 12 years before, the Canucks had
made the Stanley Cup championship against a team from

New York. And once again, their team was the heavy under-dog. Led by their captain, Mark Messier, the New York Rangers had won the President's Trophy as the first-place team in the NHL, finishing with 112 points — 27 more than Vancouver. In their only other Stanley Cup final appearance in 1982, the Canucks had lost four straight to the New York Islanders. Many believed a similar fate awaited the team this time.

But in hockey, a hot goalie can steal a series. In game one, Kirk McLean faced 54 Rangers' shots. Blueliner Bret Hedican, one of Quinn's late season acquisitions, scored the Canucks' first goal. Martin Gelinas, a player plucked off the waiver wire from Quebec in January, scored on a deflection with just 60 seconds remaining in the third period. The game went to sudden-death overtime. Then Greg Adams scored at 19:26 of overtime. It was the Canucks' sixth overtime victory in the playoffs that season.

The Rangers won the next three games, taking a 3-1 series lead, thanks to defenceman Brian Leetch, who scored four goals in 180 minutes of hockey. In game five, with the Stanley Cup inside Madison Square Garden, the never-say-die Canucks looked to spoil a Broadway-sized celebration. Defenceman Jeff Brown's goal gave the Canucks a 1-0 lead after two periods. They built up an insurmountable-look-ing 3-0 lead early in the third before the Rangers tied the game at 3-3. Dave Babych scored the game-winner at 9:31 of the third. "It looked like the Rangers were going to the Cup and then Babych scored and the Canucks win it 4-3 so coming home, everybody's all pumped up," recalled a relieved Robson.

Game six turned out to be the most exciting game ever played at the Pacific Coliseum. Facing elimination for the fifth time in the 1994 playoffs, Geoff Courtnall provided the Canucks with another pivotal playoff moment. With less than two minutes remaining in the third period, the Victoria native scored what appeared to be his second goal of the night, making the score 4-1. But the red light failed to come on and the play continued. The Rangers went back down the ice and captain Mark Messier scored on a confused-looking McLean with 58 seconds remaining. The referee believed Courtnall's shot had hit the crossbar, so he hadn't blown the whistle. "We were high on the east side doing radio and Tom Larscheid and I could see the puck definitely went in and out and the official didn't stop the play. Everybody knew it was in and then the Rangers score," recalled Robson. Fortunately for the Canucks, the 1994 playoffs marked the first year the NHL used video review. After Messier's tap-in had apparently made it a one-goal game, NHL officials replayed Courtnall's phantom goal. It counted, and as Robson described, "The place goes crazy. From a Canucks' standpoint, certainly the game six of '94 was the best ever."

Jeff Brown added two goals during the game. At one point in the game, *Hockey Night in Canada* TV cameras zoomed in on Petr Nedved, who was in the stands at the Pacific Coliseum. Seeing this, fans chanted, "Thank you,

Petr," in reference to the fact that Brown, along with Hedican and La Fayette, had come to Vancouver in exchange for the Czech. After the game, Pat Quinn told Eric Duhatschek that those three players Nedved fetched had helped put the Canucks in contention for the Cup. "We like Petr. I didn't want to ever lose him. But those things happen and we were fortunate to get the three kids we did. They really filled out our roster and gave us depth. I don't think it's any secret — without that depth we wouldn't be here today."

It was back to Gotham City for game seven. The Rangers got off to a 2-0 lead and the Canucks' chances of a Stanley Cup victory looked bleak. At 5:21 of the second period, though, Trevor Linden scored a shorthanded goal. New York restored their two-goal advantage when Mark Messier scored on the power play. Linden, playing his most dominant game in a Canucks jersey, scored again at 4:30 of the third period. But the closest the Canucks came to tie the game pinged off the crossbar. Nathan La Fayette took a pass from Courtnall and backhanded the puck past goalie Mike Richter only to hit the iron.

Geoff Courtnall, although he had won a Stanley Cup with Edmonton, said the 1994 run in his native British Columbia remains a career highlight. He had scored a Canucks record of three game-winning goals. Did the stick with which he scored the game five winner against Calgary have a legal curve? During a *Hockey Night in Canada* interview that never aired, Robson asked Courtnall about the curve on his Easton.

"I said, 'You mean that you won that game with an illegal stick?' He said, 'But nobody checked in overtime.'"

Chapter 7
Markus Naslund: Dizzy Heights

he swap of disappointing draft choices hardly made newspaper headlines in Vancouver. Markus Naslund came to the Canucks on March 20, 1996, when general manager Pat Quinn sent his team's 1991 first-round pick, Alex Stojanov, to the Penguins. Naslund had asked for a trade from Pittsburgh after being moved off the club's top unit. "I really want out of here and I'm happy to be in Vancouver," Naslund said after the deadline deal. "It took a while. I'm looking forward to getting more chances to play and a fresh, new start."

He had been drafted to score goals. The Pittsburgh Penguins used their first choice, 16th overall, at the 1991 NHL Entry Draft to select Naslund. General manager Craig Patrick had every reason to believe he'd added another sniper to a

Stanley Cup dynasty-in-the-making. That May, the Penguins had hoisted the Stanley Cup and the team looked poised for another set of diamond-encrusted championship rings. Naslund was supposed to add more firepower to a team that already boasted the likes of Mario Lemieux and Czech rookie sensation Jaromir Jagr.

Patrick liked Naslund's strong hockey pedigree. The talented left-winger grew up in Ornskoldsvik, a small pulp and paper town on the east coast of Sweden famous for exporting talented players to the NHL. As a young boy, Naslund dreamed about playing in the NHL, just like his idol Hakan Loob, who won a Stanley Cup with the Calgary Flames in 1989. During his peewee years, Naslund played against another future NHLer, Peter Forsberg. "It was basically me against Peter," Naslund said, recalling the first time playing against Forsberg. "I think we won 9-8 and we both scored seven goals."

The two players would be arch-rivals until Naslund turned 16 and both began playing for the same junior hockey club. Born just 10 days apart, the pair have been friends, teammates, or competitors ever since. At the 1993 World Junior Championship in Gavle, Sweden, Naslund played on a line with Forsberg and Niklas Sundstrom. He led the competition with goals and finished second in assists and points. His 13 goals still stand as a tournament record.

But the NHL would have to wait. Before joining the Penguins, Naslund — like many Swedish players — decided to hone his skills at home. Playing for the powerful club MoDo with old pal Forsberg, he scored 22 goals and 39 points during the 1992-93 season. Having proven himself in the Swedish Elite League, the 5-foot-11, 195-pounder figured he was then ready for the NHL.

Joining the Pittsburgh Penguins prior to the 1993-94 season, the highly touted Swede struggled to acclimatize himself in the NHL. The players were bigger, the ice surface was smaller, and the intensity much greater than in the Swedish game. He made his rookie debut on October 5, 1993 against the Philadelphia Flyers. It took more than a month for the young winger to score his first NHL goal during a 3-3 tie on the road against the St. Louis Blues. Naslund dressed for 71 games in his rookie season and recorded only four goals and 11 assists. His sophomore campaign didn't prove to be any more satisfying. During the lockout-shortened 1994-95 campaign, he dressed for 14 games with the Pens, registering two goals and two assists.

As Naslund would later admit, his inauspicious start in the NHL forced him to face a type of on-ice adversity he wasn't prepared for. "It was the first time in my whole career that I didn't have any success. I was used to being the star or at least one of the better players. All of the sudden, I was on the fourth line and they didn't even care if I dressed."

Naslund seriously contemplated zipping up his hockey bag and returning to the more familiar Swedish Elite League. But, wanting to prove he belonged in the NHL alongside other elite players like Forsberg, he returned for another season. The start of the 1995-96 season looked like it might be a breakthrough campaign for the forward. Playing on a line with superstar Lemieux, Naslund showed flashes of the brilliance he'd shown as a youngster. In 66 games, he'd netted 19 goals and 33 assists. But after being demoted from the Lemieux line in December, the 22-year-old winger was again questioning his future with the Pens.

While Naslund struggled to find his NHL scoring touch, countryman and friend Forsberg seemed born to play in the NHL. In the lockout-shortened 1994-95 season, Forsberg scored 15 goals and 35 assists and won the Calder Trophy as the league's top rookie. Forsberg finished the 1995-96 season with 30 goals and 86 assists in 82 games. He was fifth overall in NHL scoring. Naslund, meanwhile, hoped a change of locale to Vancouver would jumpstart his floundering NHL career.

In 10 regular-season games with the Canucks, Naslund managed only three goals — a hat trick versus the Calgary Flames on April 13. In the first round of the Stanley Cup playoffs, Naslund would then face-off against Forsberg and the Colorado Avalanche. The Avs beat the Canucks in six games. In his first-ever playoff appearance, Naslund scored a goal and two assists. Forsberg, meanwhile, scored 10 goals and 11 assists as the Avs went on to sip bubbly from Lord Stanley's Cup.

During the 1996-97 season, Naslund fired a career-high

21 goals, finishing fifth among the Canucks with 41 points. He tied for second on the team with four game-winners. That summer, he looked forward to returning to the rink. But, after the team's pitiable start to the 1997-98 season, GM Quinn and coach Tom Renney were both replaced.

Mike Keenan, an intolerant coach with a short fuse, scrutinized Naslund's play and found it wanting. He almost immediately benched the winger. On January 5, Naslund returned to the ice after three straight games as a healthy scratch. He scored a goal and an assist in a 3-2 victory over the Los Angles Kings. Although he was back in the lineup, he still had a lot to prove to Keenan, who'd publicly questioned the Swede's intensity. Naslund voiced his own displeasure over his lack of playing time to local reporters. He'd started the season on the first line but he was dropping fast. A headline in the *Vancouver Sun* read: "Naslund asks to play — anywhere: The Vancouver Canucks forward informed the team he'd like a trade if he cannot get regular ice time."

It was a difficult time for Naslund who, at times, appeared lost on the ice. He finished the season with 14 goals and 20 assists. His future in Vancouver was far from certain. During the off-season, he and close friend Adrian Aucoin, a Canucks defenceman also suffering from Keenan's wrath, went on a fishing trip in Sweden. Naslund confided to the blueliner that he was considering another trade request.

Naslund started the 1998-99 season on the fourth line with Brandon Convery and converted defenceman Bert

Robertsson — hardly the type of creative linemates that would allow Naslund to display his offensive skills. Again Naslund searched for answers. "My first year here, he was very frustrated," recalled Brian Burke. "We had a slow start and Mike Keenan was here and he wasn't getting the proper ice time and he was very frustrated. I sat down with him and said, 'Look Markus, it's a new situation and you have to be patient.' He did not ask for a trade or bitch about his ice time or bitch about anything. He was just very frustrated because the puck wasn't going in. I got several trade offers for Markus my first year so I sat down with him and said, 'I'm not trading you Markus. If things don't improve for you here, there might be a coaching change in the future but you're not going anywhere.'"

Then fate intervened: Alexander Mogilny suffered a knee sprain. It moved Naslund to the Canucks' top line with Mark Messier and rugged right winger Brad May. "Keenan had no alternative but to play Markus, he didn't have anyone else so he had to play him, he kept throwing him out and Markus just thrived," Gallagher recalled. Naslund made the most of the opportunity, scoring 19 points in the next 13 games. His game was finally reflecting the offensive potential scouts had projected years earlier. "Mike pushed him and goaded him, and to some degree Naslund believes that a lot of that pushing and goading helped," said Gallagher. Keenan's tough-love approach had, after all, jumpstarted the flat-lining careers of future all-stars Chris Pronger and Joe Thornton. "At the same time, in the back of Markus's mind, he always felt that all he needed was a chance to get on the ice. And it took injuries for that to happen," Gallagher added.

Naslund finished the season with a career-high 36 goals and 66 points. Playing with Messier most of the season, he averaged 20 minutes of ice time and took 205 shots on net. His play earned him a spot on the World Team for the 1999 NHL all-star game in Tampa. Naslund's confidence and ice time grew exponentially. He was having fun again, and with it came points. In 1999-00, he led the Canucks in scoring with 27 goals and 38 assists. Naslund surfaced as one of the team's brightest offensive talents and as a leader in the locker room.

With so many top Swedes on their roster, the Canucks held their 2000-01 pre-season training camp in Stockholm, Sweden. The return of Mark Messier to the Rangers had left the Canucks without a captain. Burke told Coach Crawford he had to come back to him with a recommendation for team captain. The coaching staff went around and around, never coming up with a different name. "They talked about Todd [Bertuzzi] they talked about Jovo [Ed Jovanovski], but it kept coming back to Markus. So we met in my hotel suite and Crow said, 'We're naming Markus captain,' and I said, 'Good for you, I think it's a great choice.'" On September 15, 2000, Markus Naslund became the first Swedish captain of the Canucks.

Naslund appeared comfortable shouldering the burden

of the "C" stitched on his jersey. He scored a career-high 41 goals — the most ever scored by a Canucks captain — despite suffering a season-ending broken leg on March 16. Naslund's remarkable season helped the Canucks to their first playoff encounter in five seasons. Unfortunately, without Naslund in the lineup, the Colorado Avalanche swept the plucky but undermanned Canucks.

Naslund's on-ice ascendancy earned him a new contract in the summer of 2001. Vancouver Canucks president and general manager Brian Burke announced that the team had extended their star captain's contract through the 2004-05 season. Naslund, who had one year remaining on his previous deal, had agreed to a three-year extension. "We're very pleased to reach this long term agreement with Markus," Burke said. "He has demonstrated the class, integrity, and leadership required to be a great captain in this league, and we couldn't ask for a better person to lead the Canucks into the future."

After signing his name on a contract that paid him more than US$5 million per season, Naslund registered another career-best campaign in 2001-02. He finished second in the NHL's Art Ross race with 90 points in 81 games. He also became the only player in franchise history to lead the league in scoring after January 1 and was named to the NHL's first all-star team by fan balloting. He didn't disappoint, netting a hat trick and an assist, while being named the game's second star.

"Nazzy," as he's known to his teammates, was also making the players on his line better. In 2002-03, Todd Bertuzzi scored a career-high 97 points and 46 goals. The line's centre, Brendan Morrison, was also flourishing, establishing career highs with 25 goals and 46 assists. "I'm in a situation in which I can accomplish things — Markus has made me a more patient player," linemate Bertuzzi told *Sports Illustrated*. "Before, I'd want to get the puck off my stick as soon as possible. Markus saw me differently, as a guy with skill. Now I'm holding onto the puck, using the extra second to do something creative."

Besides raising the level of his teammate's play, Naslund was also earning recognition as one of the NHL's elite players. At the 2003 NHL Players Association (NHLPA) awards luncheon held in the Hockey Hall of Fame, Naslund made hockey history. A 10-year NHL veteran at 29, he had enjoyed another career season with the Vancouver Canucks. Blessed with one of the league's best wrist shots, the flashy left-winger had scored 48 times and added 56 assists for a career-high 104 points. Naslund had also established a new single-game career high when he scored a goal and added five assists against the Atlanta Thrashers on February 25. He led all NHL sharpshooters with 12 game-winning goals and 56 power-play points. Had it not been for boyhood friend Peter Forsberg, who scored a hat trick on the final day of the NHL regular season, Naslund would have captured the league's scoring derby. Instead, he finished two points behind

Forsberg, who netted 29 goals and 77 assists. Naslund finished runner-up for the Art Ross Trophy — awarded to the top point-producer in the NHL during the regular season — for the second straight season.

Still, none of that mattered. Senator Frank Mahovlich, a member of the Hockey Hall of Fame, presented Naslund with the 2003 Lester B. Pearson Award as the most outstanding player during the NHL regular season. Named after the former prime minister, the award had been handed out since 1970-71. Boston Bruins forward Phil Esposito is the first name on a list of winners that includes the game's greatest stars. Wayne Gretzky won the award five times. Mario Lemieux's name is engraved on the trophy four times. As the other two nominees, Forsberg and Joe Thornton of the Boston Bruins, applauded him, Naslund collected the hardware dressed in a dapper beige suit, blue shirt, and matching tie. He became the first Vancouver Canuck and the first Swedish-born player to win the prestigious award.

For Naslund, like the recipients before him, receiving recognition from his opponents was the highlight of collecting the award. "I can honestly say this one is special, even though it doesn't get the publicity the Hart Trophy gets," Naslund said earnestly. "It's still a neat thing when your peers vote for you." One of the players who voted for Naslund was Forsberg, who told reporters, "I think he had a great year. He deserved it."

Naslund talked to reporters about the indelible imprint

Marcus Naslund

that playing on a line with former Canucks captain Mark Messier, a two-time winner of the Pearson award, made on his career. "Anytime you're around greatness, which I look at him [Messier] being, I think you try to pick up things. Just trying to see how he tried to keep the team tight, not only on the ice but off the ice, that's the stuff that you try to remember," Naslund said.

The dizzy heights of glory Naslund experienced that muggy June afternoon in Toronto stood in stark contrast to the high-altitude sickness he had once suffered as a healthy scratch — watching his teammates from the GM Place press box. After several disappointing seasons, Naslund had at last fulfilled the potential that ranked him among the elite prospects prior to the 1991 Draft.

Along with the recognition from his peers, Naslund had also become one of the league's most marketable superstars. In 2003, Nike Canada selected Naslund as one of the stars of the company's "Light It Up" campaign. The television commercials were designed to inspire young players to embrace a more offensive style of play and to foster excitement about the beauty of the game of hockey. In one 60-second spot, the talented left-winger chases a puck out of the hockey arena onto a busy street, down an alleyway, and into a hotel restaurant kitchen. He crashes through a plate-glass window of a hotel lobby and then grabs a cab back to the hockey rink. Nike Canada spokesman Derek Kent said, "We chose Naslund as a Nike athlete because he represents what the Light It Up campaign is all about: bringing creativity and offense back into the game. That is what he does for the Canucks every time he laces his [skates] up."

Naslund also answers the tough questions each time he

unlaces his skates.

Vancouver fans adore Naslund's candor. Vancouver sportswriters throng to No. 19's locker stall — win, lose or draw. Unlike his linemate Bertuzzi's antagonistic rapport with local reporters, or some of his other teammates' penchant for platitudes, Naslund can be counted on for an honest, articulate summation of the game.

On the final day of the 2003 season, the Canucks lost to the Los Angeles Kings, giving the Colorado Avs the division title and Peter Forsberg the Art Ross Trophy. Naslund bluntly told the fans: "As you can see, we're pretty upset. We choked. We'll play a lot better in the playoffs." While many local pundits accused the Canucks of trying to get Naslund the puck in that game so he could win the Art Ross Trophy, Naslund said he wasn't concerned about personal awards. "I would have been perfectly happy had we won the division and that was my goal today."

Following a disappointing loss to the Minnesota Wild in the second round of the 2003 Stanley Cup playoffs, Naslund finally trumped his old friend Peter Forsberg. On the final day of the next (2003-4) season, he scored his 35th goal of the season. The Canucks defeated the Edmonton Oilers 5-2, ending the Avs' nine-year reign as Northwest Division champions. "We're happy about winning the [Northwest Division] title but we all know that's not what we're playing for," Naslund told a crush of reporters around his stall after the game.

Despite suffering a hyper-extended elbow February

16, and losing linemate Todd Bertuzzi on March 8 to a season-ending suspension, Naslund finished the season with 84 points in 78 games. It was his sixth-straight season as the team's top point-producer.

The Canucks' title-clinching victory set up a first-round playoff match-up against the Calgary Flames. The hard-hat team had finished three spots behind the Canucks in the West. Superstitious Canucks fans seemed delighted about the first-round match-up. The last time the teams had met in the playoffs in 1994, the Canucks won a seven-game series and advanced to the Stanley Cup final for the first time in a dozen years.

But after a series-opening 5-3 victory, the Canucks' season again ended in bitter disappointment. The Flames prevailed in a seventh-game overtime thriller on a goal by former Canuck Martin Gelinas.

The dispiriting loss and looming NHL labour dispute led to considerable speculation. Naslund, in his final year of a contract with the team, may have played his final game in a Canucks uniform. Naslund had intimated in the past that he might not sign another NHL contract. Would he return to Sweden to play in the Swedish Elite League and raise his three young children? Naslund admitted that 2003-04 had been the most draining season in his career due to his injury, the Bertuzzi incident, and all the media scrutiny. He told reporters his future in Vancouver depended on the NHL and NHLPA signing a new collective bargaining agreement in the summer. "I've got one more year on my deal and if there's a season, I'm definitely planning on coming back."

If not, Naslund's last assist as a member of the Vancouver Canucks will be replayed for years to come. With the Canucks trailing the Flames 2-1 in the dying seconds of game seven, Naslund rushed the puck from inside his own blueline. With just 5.7 seconds left on the clock and barely any fans in their seats, he deked his way in front of the Calgary net. His shot was banged in by linemate Matt Cooke to tie the game. Burke commented, "For that rush, there's only three or four guys in the National Hockey League that can make that play and he's one of them. It was just electrifying."

Chapter 8
Brian Burke: The GM Back in Place

he news was blunt and jarring, like a two-handed crosscheck. Orca Bay Sports and Entertainment had ended popular Pat Quinn's 10-year stint as hockey boss. "John McCaw and the ownership of the Vancouver Canucks have stated their desire to field a Stanley Cup competitor, but others have expressed concern about where we're at," Orca Bay deputy chairman Stan McCammon announced.

The most successful era in Vancouver Canucks history wound up abruptly as disbelieving Canucks fans heard the news on November 4, 1997. To make matters worse, Orca Bay officials didn't have a replacement candidate for Canucks general manager and president in mind. Instead, interim GM duties were spread between Orca Bay senior vice- president Stephen Bellringer, manager of hockey operations Steve Tambellini, and assistant GM Mike Penny. Nine days later, mercurial coach Mike Keenan was hired to replace Tom Renney. The power structure of the Canucks' organization was confused further.

Just as fans attempted to reconcile the fact that the Griffiths family-run Canucks had morphed into a cold-hearted corporation, they were jolted again. On January 2, the team traded goaltender Kirk McLean and hardworking forward Martin Gelinas — two heroes from the 1994 Stanley Cup final team. Later that month, Keenan continued the ignominious disbanding of the 1994 team by trading Vancouver fan favourites, Trevor Linden and Gino Odjick, to the New York Islanders. The Canucks, for years the laughingstock of the NHL because of inept management, poor records, and dubious uniform choices, had become a joke once more.

A decade after hiring Quinn away from the Los Angles Kings, the Canucks were again in a desperate search for a new hockey boss to lead the team back to the top of the standings. Handicapping the list of candidates for the general manager vacancy, *Vancouver Sun* reporter Mike Beamish included former Canucks vice-president and director of hockey operations Brian Burke with Cliff Fletcher, Mike Keenan, John Muckler, and Mike Gillis. Beside Burke's bio, Beamish wrote: "Anyone familiar with Burke's competitive nature knows he's spinning his wheels at the head office in New York, and he dearly would love another shot a building a team, as he did with middling results in Hartford." But, Beamish continued knowingly, "He might be too much of a loose cannon for those corporate, image-is-everything folks at Orca Bay."

Not long ago, visitors walking through the lobby of Gate 5 at General Motors Place were greeted by a photograph of Brian Burke taken during his playing days in the American Hockey League — bearded and helmet-less, blood rushing down his face. The image epitomized Burke's approach to the game, both as a player and more recently as a hockey executive. "I think belligerence is an asset ... show me a successful person who didn't stubbornly adhere to what they believed in. Successful people believe in themselves and don't back down," Burke said.

Fortunately, reclusive Vancouver Canucks owner John McCaw, who'd made his fortune in the telecommunications industry, had the sense to telephone Brian Burke. Burke seemed eager to return to Vancouver, despite getting advice to the contrary. Although former Canucks GM Pat Quinn had been positive about the Vancouver hockey market, most GMs in the NHL fraternity believed employment in Canada posed a much greater challenge — a weaker Canadian dollar and more critical press. "I was advised by people I really respect not to even think about the Vancouver job, but I knew the city and I knew the market and I knew it was one of the greatest hockey towns in the world and I love Vancouver," Burke said.

Vancouver Canucks

The official announcement of Brian Burke's hiring on June 22, 1998, heralded a new sheriff in town. He wasn't shooting blanks. "I want to be crystal clear about this, I have been given authority over the entire hockey operation," Burke said at a press conference held in the bowels of GM Place. He had arrived sporting a pair of Vancouver Canucks cufflinks that had been given to him during his going-away party in 1992. But he knew he'd have to roll up his sleeves in order to turn the fortunes of the floundering club around.

To shape the Canucks into a more competitive team on the ice, Burke also knew he would first have to make the team more competitive off the ice. In 1998, the high-salaried last-place team had lost $36 million while playing in front of rows of empty seats. Their season ticket base was around 7000. "When I got here, this team was bleeding red ink, not just leaking red ink, it was gushing," he recalled. "To me there was no alternative but for somebody to come in here and say, 'We're not going to run this like somebody's hobby; we are going to run this like a business.'"

Burke's hockey resume made him the perfect man for the job. Born in Rhode Island and raised in Minnesota, Burke didn't start playing hockey until he was 13. Despite what he called "limited ability," he managed to crack the Providence College team as a walk-on. He later earned a full scholarship and the team captaincy. After Providence, Burke signed with the Philadelphia Flyers. He played for the team's American Hockey League farm club, the Maine Mariners, during the

1977-78 season. The Mariners won the Calder Cup and Burke was undefeated in 10 fights, racking up three goals and five assists in 65 games. He knew, however, that his skill level had taken him as far as he could get on the ice. He decided to hit the books instead, gaining acceptance to Harvard Law School. He practiced law for six years in Boston as a player agent. Then he received a call from a man he'd gotten to know in the Philadelphia organization, the same man to whom he'd later loaned his law books — Pat Quinn.

Quinn had been hired in 1987 by Arthur Griffiths to rebuild the perpetually struggling Vancouver franchise that had just finished its 11th season in a row under .500. Quinn's first move was to hire Burke as his vice-president and director of hockey operations. Burke was put in charge of the team's scouting system, its farm team, and negotiating all players contracts. In five seasons, the pair of Irishmen built a 59-point bottom dweller into a 96-point Smythe Division champion. "He gave me my first shot here and I'm forever grateful for that," Burke said of his mentor Quinn.

Burke returned to Vancouver to take over Quinn's job as president and general manager of the Canucks in the summer of 1998. The tough-talking Irishman didn't back down from anyone: the local press, opposing general managers, NHL officials, player agents, and — occasionally — his own players. And while his blunt personality annoyed some people, he was also the most sought-after quote in the NHL. A sample of Burke's most memorable smart bombs:

On rookie goalie Alex Auld becoming starter Dan Cloutier's backup for the 2003-04 season: "There's no way that Alex Auld was going to be on the team this year unless he flew to France during the summer and bathed in the holy waters at Lourdes."

On unrestricted free-agent winger Trent Klatt: "If Trent can get three years at over a million dollars from someone else, God bless him, I'll drive him to the airport."

On the officiating during the Canucks' first-round series against the Detroit Red Wings in the 2002 Western Conference quarter final: "I want to point out that Todd Bertuzzi does not play for Detroit. It just looks like it because he's wearing two or three red sweaters all the time."

On the media: "We never start these fights. Like a general manager never wakes up and says, 'Hey who can I fight with today in the media?' We pick up the newspaper and read some garbage story that should be at the bottom of a bird cage, or wrapping a fish, or in the corner of a kitchen for a puppy ... and if it's something about our hockey team that is untrue or unfair ... we fly off the handle and react."

On Pavel Bure's trade request: "The inmates don't run the asylum. If a player wants to be traded, that's fine but he's got a contract to play here. And the only way a player gets traded in my organization, is if it upgrades my organization."

On Burke himself: "I think fans would agree, whether they like me or hate me, that when I'm talking, I'm telling the truth. It may not be what they want to hear. I don't have media consultants. It's me."

Burke's bombastic quotes marked a welcome departure from the usual formal GM-speak of the NHL. The fact that the tough-talking Burke backed up his words made him one of the most successful general managers in the history of the Vancouver franchise. Burke's return to the West Coast was greeted by both the local hockey fandom and hockey beat reporters much like the triumphant return of a sheriff to a lawless frontier. Even for a hockey franchise rich in misadventure and dubious uniform design, the seven months that preceded Burke's arrival represented the nadir of the modern-era Canucks.

Vancouver was Burke's biggest challenge as a hockey executive. He inherited a last-place team in complete disarray. The Canucks finished the 1997-98 season with a pitiful 64 points — seventh overall in the Pacific Division and second-worst overall in the entire league. Not even the off-season free-agent signing of Mark Messier, a player expected to take the Canucks deep into the Stanley Cup playoffs, helped. To make matters worse, Pavel Bure, the club's first and only 60-goal scorer, desperately wanted to be traded. "It was a tough first month on the job," Burke admitted. "Your superstar says, 'I don't want to play here anymore,' and we lost Jyrki Lumme that summer too. We lost one of our best defencemen and our best forward."

Most troubling to Burke, however, was the prevailing perception of the team as overpaid and underachieving.

"The team had totally lost touch with the community and the business community. To me it was, 'OK we can't fix the product right away, to turn a team around takes time but we can certainly address the other two issues.'" Burke, a tireless worker who only takes time off on St. Patrick's Day, began a hockey blitzkrieg. He met with season ticket holders, held town meetings, attended chamber of commerce meetings, and agreed to speaking engagements. "I was doing three or four of those a day," recalled Burke. Canucks players, meanwhile, stepped off the ice and into the community. They campaigned for literacy, visited hospitals and schools, and showed they cared.

Growing up in a large, Irish Catholic family may have made Burke belligerent, but it also taught him the value of a dollar. Running a Canadian-market team, Burke realized he'd have to fight hard to save money in order to stay economically viable in a Canadian market. The Diet Coke-sipping GM began watching the Canucks' operating budget as closely as the calories in his soft drinks. After arriving in Vancouver, he began trimming player payroll while improving the team in the standings — something believed impossible by most free-spending NHL general managers. That's not to say, however, that Burke the businessman wasn't sometimes at odds with Burke the hockey man. "The way the sports model works is the GM wants to improve the product so he spends more money. We had to improve the product while we spent less money," he explained. The decision not to exercise the option on Mark Messier's $6 million contract was gut-wrenchingly difficult, but Burke felt the team couldn't afford the salary. He also had to unload high-priced Soviet superstar Alex Mogilny in a trade to New Jersey in exchange for Brendan Morrison and Denis Pederson. The decision was again based on the economics of the game.

Paying his players not a penny more than fair market value was a philosophy Burke had adopted when he worked as Pat Quinn's chief contract negotiator. Vancouver player agent Ron Perrick remembered sitting across from Burke at the negotiation table during his first stint with the Canucks. "What you see is what you get with Brian. If he thinks he's right, he's not going to pussy foot around. He does his homework and makes you work for every inch," said Perrick, whose NHL clients include Cliff Ronning and Rod Brind'Amour.

Burke made no apologies for his hardball negotiating tactics. "The players have to fight for the money here. Our philosophy is to pay what is fair, but if you pay players a penny more than market value then you've wasted a penny."

Paying fair market value wasn't the only way he kept the team's payroll manageable. Burke could tell you down to the nickel exactly what it costs to take a cab from GM Place to the airport. He could also tell you that if he's going on an overnight business trip, it's cheaper for him drive to the Vancouver airport and pay for overnight parking. If the trip is longer than three days, it's less expensive to take a cab and leave his SUV parked at the rink. "That's how closely we watch the money here," he said.

To turn the Canucks around a second time, working in a much chillier NHL economic climate for Canadian teams, Burke relied heavily on lessons learned from his two biggest hockey mentors, Quinn and Lou Lamoriello. At Providence, Burke had been coached by the longstanding New Jersey Devils president and general manager Lamoriello. Burke claimed, "In terms of the modern era on how to put a team together, Lamoriello is the architect. If you can't create massive revenues and you have to keep an eye on what you spend, you don't have a choice, you've got to watch those costs and contain them."

As a player's agent, Burke was equally cost conscious, refusing to take on clients who didn't abide by his prescribed budget limit on what players could spend on new cars and clothes with their first NHL contracts. "You hire me, I work hourly, and you agree to these rules in terms of budget, or you get somebody else," Burke explained to prospective clients. One year, when the dollar limit for a new car happened to be $14,000, according to the "Burke Rules," Winnipeg rookie Peter Taglianetti called his agent from a Saab dealership. The young defenceman told Burke he'd talked the car dealer down to $14,400. "Can I buy the car?" he asked. "I said, put the dealer on the phone," Burke recalled. "The car dealer gets on the phone and I said, 'In 30 seconds you're either selling him that car for $14,000 or he's walking out the door. He says 'OK.' Peter gets back on the phone and I say, 'You're OK for the budget this year.'"

However, Burke knew that fiscal responsibility alone wouldn't put fans in the seats at GM Place. Burke's first major move as GM in Vancouver was the January 1999 blockbuster trade that sent petulant Soviet star Pavel Bure to the Florida Panthers for Ed Jovanovski and others. The deal he made one week later may have been the seminal moment in turning around the franchise, though.

On January 24, 1999, Burke hired Marc Crawford, a coach who had won the Stanley Cup as the bench boss of the Colorado Avalanche in 1996. In 1994, "Crow," as he was known, had been named the youngest recipient of the Jack Adams trophy, awarded to the league's top coach. "I think bringing Crow in was a huge step toward bringing the credibility of the franchise back; not only did it get rid of the unpopular Mike Keenan, but people knew Crow as a winner."

Burke and Crawford also could agree on a style of hockey they wanted the team to play. When he interviewed Crawford, Burke reiterated that he didn't want to play the suffocating, defensive brand of hockey that had become in vogue in the NHL. "I wanted to play an entertaining style, no trap, no left-wing lock, none of that crap, I want to skate. I want to trade chances. In Canada, fans don't want to watch the trap. You're not going to get them into the building playing a conservative style. We played a run-and-gun entertaining style," Burke said.

Burke's blueprint for building a strong organization also called for developing a strong nucleus and farm system through the draft. When Burke left the Canucks to take over the floundering Hartford Whalers during the 1992-93 season, he had started the team's rebuilding process with a blockbuster deal on draft day. It landed him Chris Pronger, a defenceman who had matured into a Norris Trophy-calibre blueliner. Burke again made a headline-grabbing deal at the 1999 NHL Entry Draft in Tampa. He acquired the second and third overall picks in order to take Daniel and Henrik Sedin.

In 1999-2000, Burke's team enjoyed a 25-point turnaround. One season later, the Canucks qualified for the Stanley Cup playoffs for the first time in four seasons. In 2001, fellow GMs voted him the *Sporting News* NHL Executive of the Year. By 2002-03, the moves Burke made on and off the ice had managed to improve his club's points for the fourth consecutive season. Finishing with a club-record 104 points, the Canucks also made the playoffs for the third straight year. Burke had managed to cut losses significantly, getting the payroll to a more manageable level. He improved the quality of the game on the ice, which led to an increase in the season ticket base in 2003.

At the start of the 2003-04 season, Burke's playoff-tested Canucks set out for their ultimate goal — the Stanley Cup. Focus shifted away from the team in February, however. Burke made newspaper headlines and lit up the phone boards at local radio call-in shows after he described himself as a "lame-duck GM." Burke, of course, was referring to the fact that his contract with the Canucks would expire on July 1, 2004. Stan McCammon, the CEO of Orca Bay Sports and Entertainment, said the Canucks' ownership would deal with Burke's contract at the end of the season. Such assurances didn't assuage the displeasure of the fans. They feared losing the architect of the dramatic franchise turnaround. One fan started a Web site called signbrianburke.com, imploring fans to sign an online petition for the club to re-sign Burke. An online survey conducted by the *Vancouver Sun* showed that 75.6 of respondents wanted Burke back at the helm.

Burke's Irish bluster would ostensibly cost him his job as the president and general manager of the Vancouver Canucks. After an unexpected first-round exit in the 2004 Stanley Cup finals to the Calgary Flames, Seattle-based billionaire John McCaw decided not to renew Burke's contract. McCammon declined to talk to the media about why Brian Burke's contract had not been renewed. Many speculated that the fractious relationship between the two men led to the Canucks boss's dismissal. "I think I've had a very good relationship with Brian. That has no play in this decision," countered McCammon. "Brian's probably done as masterful a job in taking a franchise that was in the position we're in and turning it [around]. Obviously, in doing so, he's had a great deal of support from a variety of people, but at the end of the day, he's the one, to use his [Burke's] term, who had the hands on the wheel.'"

After the firing of Brian Burke, it was the media's turn to be belligerent. "Either there's a problem between Burke and McCammon or Orca Bay just dumped the best GM in franchise history on a whim. Given this market's investment in this team, it deserved some kind — any kind come to think of it — of explanation on Monday," wrote *Province* columnist Ed Willes.

Vancouver Sun columnist Gary Mason also seethed over the firing of one of the hockey club's most successful and popular general managers with no explanation from ownership: "Well, let me say the whole thing stinks. The decision, the pathetically weak and cowardly response by ownership, the whole thing. It's like the day they fired Pat Quinn, except this time they remembered to thank the guy for his years of service."

Given Burke's record as the GM of the Canucks, it seems unthinkable that he was "trumped." He arrived in Vancouver to inherit a bottom-dwelling 64-point team. Burke quickly turned the team into an 83-point playoff team in two seasons. His team made four straight playoff appearances and had back-to-back seasons of more than 100 points. The Canucks had a season ticket base of 16,600 and 86 straight sellouts. Off the ice, Burke had similar success: the introduction of pay-per-view games and a venture into a lottery partnership. Sure, Burke was often at odds with the media, and he didn't exactly fit the profile of an Orca Bay executive. But the building was sold out and the team had just won its first divisional title in 11 years.

At his final press conference with the Vancouver media, Burke wasn't his usual belligerent self, choosing instead to take the moment to thank all those who had helped him along the way. He named everyone from the Canucks' scouting staff to owner John McCaw for the opportunity to run the organization. Burke didn't mention McCammon, however, intimating that personal relationships had played a role in his demise. "Irishmen are supposed to be good at politics. I guess I'm not because I have not figured out this part of the job."

Three days after the Canucks decided not to renew Burke's contract, the organization hired his former right-hand man, Dave Nonis, as the new general manager. The ninth GM in team history must now attempt to break the curse of Black Tuesday — the day the team lost a lottery wheel spin for future Hall-of-Famer Gilbert Perreault — and bring Lord Stanley back to the West Coast for the first time since 1915.

Further Reading

Banks, Kerry. *Pavel Bure: The Riddle of the Russian Rocket.* Greystone Books, 1999.

Boyd, Denny. *The Vancouver Canucks Story.* McGraw-Hill Ryerson, 1973.

Gallagher, Tony and Gasher, Mike. *Towels, Triumph and Tears: The Vancouver Canucks and their Amazing Drive to the 1982 Stanley Cup Final.* Harbour Publishing, 1982.

Jewison, Norm. *Vancouver Canucks: The First Twenty Years.* Polestar Press Ltd., 1990.

MacIntyre, Iain. *Vancouver Canucks.* Creative Education, 1996.

Rossiter, Sean. *Vancouver Canucks: The Silver Edition.* Opus Productions Inc., 1994.

Acknowledgments

I want to thank all those who took the time to share with me their engaging stories about the Vancouver Canucks: Kerry Banks, Brian Burke, Greg Douglas, Tony Gallagher, Orland Kurtenbach, Chris Oddleifson, Gino Odjick, Jim Robson, Darcy Rota, and Tiger Williams. I would also like to acknowledge the excellent sportswriters of the *Vancouver Sun, Vancouver Province, Calgary Herald, Edmonton Journal,* and *New York Times,* for supplying many of the quotes contained in these stories. Denny Boyd's *The Vancouver Story* and *Tiger: A Hockey Story,* written by James Lawton, were also valuable sources for quotes in this book. Thanks to Michael Harling for his guidance and Trevor Doull for his exhaustive newspaper clipping library from the 1982 Stanley Cup playoffs. Special thanks to Kara Turner of Altitude for the opportunity to write this book and editor Joan Dixon for adding the varnish. Finally, I'd like to thank Heather and Graham MacKenzie for all their support.

Photo Credits

Cover: Jack Murray / Vancouver Canucks Archives; Paul Bereswill / Hockey Hall of Fame: page 29; Doug MacLellan / Hockey Hall of Fame: pages 50, 82, 92; O-Pee-Chee / Hockey Hall of Fame: page 76; Dave Sandford / Hockey Hall of Fame: page 114.

About the Author

Justin Beddall is a National Magazine Award winning writer whose mother bought him a standing-room-only ticket from a scalper to game four of the 1982 Stanley Cup final at Vancouver's Pacific Coliseum when he was 12. He has followed the team ever since. Currently a sports reporter for the *North Shore Outlook* newspaper, he has also written for *Vancouver Magazine*, the *Vancouver Sun*, and *BC Business* magazine.

also available!

ISBN 1-55153-797-4

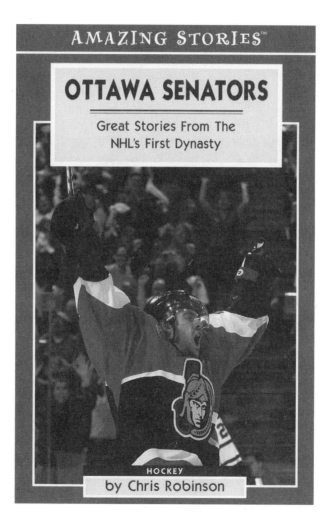

AMAZING STORIES™

CALGARY FLAMES

Fire on Ice

HOCKEY
by Monte Stewart

ISBN 1-55153-794-X

AMAZING STORIES™

EDMONTON OILERS

Stories from the
City of Champions

HOCKEY

by Rich Mole

ISBN 1-55153-798-2

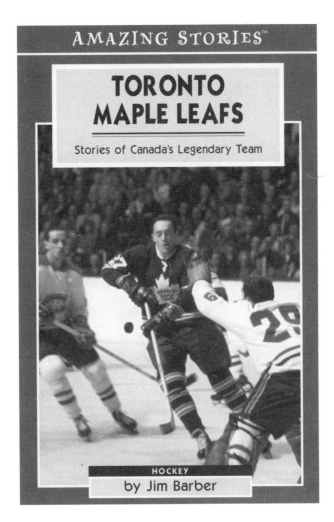

ISBN 1-55153-788-5